Adult
Children
of *Fairly*
Functional
Parents

What reviewers are saying about
Becky and Ruthie's first book,
Worms in My Tea:

Charisma

. . . the most refreshing book I've read for some time. The daughter-mother team of Freeman and Arnold is destined to be a success! This book inspires laughter.

Christian Retailing

This happy look at life—especially family life—will charm readers.

Bookstore Journal

The authors' sense of humor is comparable to Erma Bombeck's. . . . an easy-to-read experience with a touch of the profound.

Publishers Weekly

While there is humor here, there is also redemptive gentleness and a loving engagement of family process that is the essence of Mother's Day. ❧

Becky Freeman & Ruthie Arnold

Adult Children of *Fairly Functional* Parents

A Nest of My Own in the Family Tree

BROADMAN
& HOLMAN
PUBLISHERS

Nashville, Tennessee

© 1995 by Becky Freeman & Ruthie Arnold
All rights reserved

∾

Printed in the United States of America
Published by:
Broadman & Holman Publishers
Nashville, Tennessee
Design: Steven Boyd

∾

4261-55
0-8054-6155-8
Dewey Decimal Classification: 155.6
Subject Heading: Adults \ Parenting
Library of Congress Card Catalog Number: 94-37931

Scripture: Quotations marked KJV are taken from the King James Version; NASB, the New American Standard Bible, © the Lockman Foundation, 1960, 1962, 1963, 1968, 1971, 1972, 1973, 1975, 1977, used by permission; NIV, New International Version, copyright © 1973, 1978, 1984 by International Bible Society; TLB, The Living Bible, copyright © Tyndale House Publishers, Wheaton, Ill., 1971, used by permission.

Permissions: "The Wind Beneath My Wings," (Larry Henley, Jeff Silbar), © 1982 Warner House of Music & B Gold Music Corp., all rights reserved, used by permission. "I'm in Love with You, Honey," words and music by Seymour Simons, Haven Gillespie and Richard A. Whiting, copyright © 1928 (renewed) by Marlong Music, Warner Bros., Inc., and Haven Music, international copyright secured, all rights reserved, reprinted by permission. "El Shaddai," words by John Thompson and Michael Card, copyright 1982, Mole End Music. All rights on behalf of Mole End Music administered by the Sparrow Corporation; all rights reserved; used by permission.

Library of Congress Cataloging-in-Publication Data
Freeman, Becky, 1959-
    Adult children of fairly functional parents: a nest of my own in the family tree / Becky Freeman, Ruthie Arnold.
        p.   cm.
    ISBN 0-8054-6155-8
    1. Parent and adult child—United States. I. Arnold, Ruthie, 1936-
II. Title.
    HQ755.86.F74   1995
    306.874—dc20   94-37931
                                                                CIP

Dedicated in loving memory of two matriarchs of the faith:
Our Nonnie and Scott's Great-Grandma Peterson.

Contents

Acknowledgments

Writing a book about one's own family tree is a task made possible only by the encouragement and generous permission of the members who occupy its branches. And for grandparents at home with the Lord, we hope we've honored their memory, including their triumphs and their humanity.

To all our lovable and unique aunts, uncles, and cousins from all branches of the tree, we thank you profusely for the great material. An extra thanks to Etta Lynch, Ruth's sister and Becky's aunt, for her professional and detailed edit. If she hadn't encouraged us both in the early stages of writing, this book would not have become a reality.

Brothers and sisters, in-laws and out-laws, we love you for putting up with the occasional roller coaster ride that goes with being related to people who like to write.

To Becky's children, their mother would like to say thanks for putting up with Mom writing a book smack in the middle of the family living area. For at least a few weeks, you all have the privilege of watching occasional TV with the volume turned on!

We can't leave out our husbands. They've been loyal, supportive, and patient even when they had to defrost a frozen wienie for supper while we typed. Their constant belief in us helps these two female canaries keep on chirping.

To Almedia Lueg, an excellent and exacting English teacher who happens also to be a surpassingly good buddy, we say thanks for your invaluable critique and suggestions. Thanks also to Martha Moore, Gracie Malone, and Fran Sandin, all fine professional writers and dear friends who gave of their expertise at just the right time and in just the right way. And lastly, many thanks to De Lee Isbill, who read the first draft of the manuscript and by her loving way and sweet spirit encouraged us more than she knows.

And of course, to the fantastic team at Broadman & Holman—especially our fun and supportive editor, Vicki Crumpton—our sincerest thanks.

To all our friends at church and at lunch who cheer us on—your encouragement keeps us going!

At this point in these detailed acknowledgments, as Becky is getting carried away, Ruthie has asked if Becky might not want to thank the midwives who delivered her four children—and without whom we would not have all the material we need—and of course, the lovely waitress in the restaurant at lunch last week who was so gracious and made us feel we could go on.

Well, as a matter of fact, Becky does. Thank you very much. The service was superb!

Becky Freeman & Ruthie Arnold

P.S. Did we mention our first grade teachers who taught us how to write our very first words?

PART ONE

A Fledgling
in the Pecking Order

Building a Nest
of My Own

They sit on our shoulders and whisper in our ears, even when they're a thousand miles away. At times, you can't live with 'em, but there are moments when it seems you can't possibly live without 'em. The best of them hurt us at times; even the worst of them seem to manage to come through for us occasionally. How do we escape from the Omnipresent Mother?

Lately, I've been noticing an interesting phenomenon. My mother is taking over my physical body. I never thought it would happen to *moi*. Mother's calluses have appeared on my heels and her varicose veins adorn my calves, the result of some proud maternal gene with a unique sense of exterior design. (As an aside, when I ran this chapter through the spell check, it suggested I replace "vericose" with "fricassee." This is a true story.)

This morning I happened to glance in the mirror and saw my lipstick had run into the tiny new indentations around my lips. I thought for a startled moment that I saw Mother's knowing twinkle reflected back at me. When I told her about it, she seemed totally unsurprised.

"I wish I could tell you there'd never be another shock like that, but the pace is guaranteed to pick up, my dear," she observed. "As a matter of fact, I had a similar experience just last week. I had washed my hair in the kitchen and wrapped an old towel around my head to go into the bathroom to blow it dry. When I glanced in the mirror at the towel-draped lady staring back at me, I got quite a shock.

"'My goodness,' I said to the lady in the reflection, 'I'm not only beginning to look like my mother. I'm beginning to look like Mother Theresa!'"

Besides the eerie, I'm-turning-into-my-mother episodes I've been experiencing of late, I often wonder just how many times today's liberated women from all across this nation secretly find themselves needing to make a decision of grave importance—such as whether to buy one-ply or two-ply tissue—and ask themselves, "I wonder what Mother would do?" My close friend, Brenda, is head nurse for the intensive care unit at a prestigious hospital and mother to three boys. Yet she insists she cannot so much as buy a pair of panty hose without consulting her mother.

"I never go shopping without my mother," she sighed, resigned to the arrangement. "I just wait until she comes into town. I know it's codependent behavior and all, but I can't help it. The truth is, she has good taste." I happened to know that Brenda had purchased the skirt she was wearing sans her mom, and, wanting to boost her self-esteem, I complimented the skirt.

"Nice try, Beck," she said. "Mother saw this skirt on sale in Houston, called around to see if the Dallas branch stores carried them, and told me to go buy two of them in neutral shades to go with my silk paisley blouse."

What can I say? Obviously, the woman does have good taste.

In many ways, I *am* like my mother. We laugh at the same things, enjoy lingering over lunch at the cafeteria, chat about the trivial, and philosophize over the meaning of life. We both cry at romantic movies, triumphant chorales, and the emotional moment when we finally find our cars in crowded mall parking lots. However, the older I get the more I realize that, though I am definitely my mother's daughter, I am not her clone. I have made my own Declaration of Independence.

Recently when the two of us were moving through the line at the cafeteria, I brazenly overlooked the gooey fudge deserts and reached for a bowl of plain egg custard. Mother stopped and placed her hand over her heart as she struggled to recover from this moment of betrayal.

"We don't like egg custard in our family," she finally managed to say. "It's bland. It's plain. It tastes like scrambled eggs with sugar in it. It's for dull people with ulcerated stomachs. We are strong, chocolate nut women!"

Now, how could I argue with that? But since I had come this far out of the Plain Vanilla closet, I charged ahead recklessly. "Mother," I swallowed hard. "I've been wanting to tell you this for a long time. Please try to understand. You were bound to find out. And I might as well be the one to tell you. I also like—tapioca pudding."

Bewilderment clouded her eyes, but though taken aback, Mother has always tried hard to be a "with-it" kind of mom, wanting to support us in all of our decisions. Eventually she even joined me in sharing a bowl of bread pudding. So what if she smothered her half with caramel sauce. It's the gesture that counts.

That day, we began to talk about the gradual but profound changes that had been taking place in our relationship over a period of time without either of us really realizing it. We had clearly, and sometimes painfully, moved from a relationship that was primarily "mother and daughter" toward becoming good buddies.

"Sounds like there's a book in there somewhere," I mused.

"Sure would help if at least one of us was an authority," she sighed, but we decided not to let that tiny deficit hold us back. We'd write the book anyway.

"I've been around a long time," Mother said, "and you know lots of people." I could see she was getting excited.

When my relationship with my mother expanded to include professional writing, my confidence in my own judgment and ability began to increase. But I wasn't sure my mother had come to see me as a fully functional adult. I remembered a day recently when we had been on the phone, making a date for our next meeting at the cafeteria.

"It's going to be raining," she said before signing off. "You'll need a raincoat, you know. Oh, dear, there I go again." My heart skipped a beat, but *then* she added, "Oh, well. I might as well say it. Don't forget to go potty before you leave."

Obviously, this mother/friend/equal idea was going to require a little reinforcement, I decided, and today was as good a time as any. I seized the opportunity to assert myself once more. As we were finishing our spinach salads, the waitress walked by pushing the beverage cart.

"May I get you anything? A cup of coffee, perhaps?" she inquired. I waited to be sure I had Mother's full attention and then spoke with deliberate casualness.

"Yes, I'd like a cup, please." From the corner of my eye, I saw Mother sit straighter in her chair, as if she had been poked in the back by an invisible finger.

"You don't drink coffee!" she said in amazement. "You don't even *like* it!"

"I know," I replied in my most professional voice. "I'm making a unilateral decision to enjoy some anyway. I relish holding the cup and savoring the aroma. It makes me look quite sophisticated, don't you think?"

Since we had by this time committed ourselves to write a book based in part on how successful she had been in allowing her daughter to be her own person, she swallowed hard before answering, "Come to think of it, it does!" Then she smiled a wicked smile, lifted her own cup to mine in a toast, and said, "Be careful not to spill it. It's hot."

It was fun, that moment of wanton rebellion . . . that flaunting of my radical independence from all my mother thinks I am. As I sipped my coffee (which tasted like warm turpentine), my mind drifted to a mental image of our family tree. I was obviously on the road to being in emotional control of my own life, but had I truly discovered and feathered my own nest, so to speak, on a branch of that tree? Maybe through the process of writing this book with Mother, I'd discover my unique roost among its leafy boughs.

Basically, Mother and I had decided to venture out on a limb and explore our own relationship, as well as some of our relationships with members of our families both recent and in the past. We hoped that if we analyzed how these relationships have grown and changed through the years and shared some of the lessons we've learned, others might be helped in sorting their way through relationships that can be the richest, or the most painful, in our lives.

That day in the cafeteria with Mother, I decided that this just might be the most fun project I had ever participated in. In the words of Bo Pilgrim, King of Chickens, this could be "a mind-bogglin' thang."

But speaking the truth in love,
we are to grow up in all aspects.

EPHESIANS 4:15, NASB
ॐ

7

We Can't Be Pigeon-holed

When Scott and I were engaged, our premarital counselor told us we would draw a little from Scott's family of origin and take a little scoop from my own family and blend it up with our own personalities and then "ya'll will have your own special mixture." It sounded fun—like one of those tropical fruit drinks with tiny umbrellas floating gaily among the ice. As things turned out, *sometimes* it was festive. Other times it was more like one of those brewer's yeast and powdered milk concoctions— hard to swallow but probably good for us in the long run.

In a rare quiet moment not long ago, I made a quick list of ways in which Scott and I are different—just to get it clear in my head. From the volume of material I gathered, I've come to the conclusion that we're probably not even of the same phylum. He likes fruit desserts; I'm *basically* a chocolate woman. He likes shoot-'em-up Westerns or cliff-hanger adventures. I like romance or British films where even the *lips* hardly move, with lots of witty dialogue and tense relationships—that sort of thing. He likes to fill his recreational time with purposeful activity. I like to fill my recreational time being a lazy bum. Scott doesn't have a lazy bone in his body. When I relax, people question whether I have a bone in my body at all.

My husband can't function in a mess, and of course, my most creative work is done in the mountains—mountains of laundry waiting to be folded and papers waiting to be sorted. I once found a suspicious note on the kitchen counter which read, "All these people been pickin' on me and messin' me up. Please help me. Sinfully yours, House." I believe it was Scott's handwriting.

Even our church-going preferences are cause for dispute. He prefers the laid-back atmosphere of a Sunday School class. I love the music and worshipful grandeur of Big Church. He takes showers. I adore long, hot baths, and so it goes . . . Tomato. Tomahto. Potato. Potahto. But we can't call the whole thing off. We've got too much invested. Besides, as opposite as we are, we're getting awfully attached to each other.

By far the biggest difference between my husband and me with which I have to deal is this: Scott is not only *naturally* tall and thin—he works out with weights and runs for the sheer pleasure of being in shape. And I? I am short and—let's just say that I'm currently reading *Outsmarting the Female Fat Cell* for the sheer pleasure of fantasizing about what I might look like should I ever manage to outfox my sneaky cells.

I've solved and resolved this difficulty over and over again, but periodically I decide something simply *must* be done. If reading books about losing weight would somehow do the trick, I'd currently be about the size of a coffee stirrer. But just when there seemed to be no hope for us to have a meeting of the minds here, I may have stumbled onto something that will not only help me to "just do it," but actually bring us closer together as a couple.

It all began last week when I lunched with three women friends—Linda, Lori, and Mimi. Whatever possessed me to accept an invitation to dine with three women whose combined total weight is probably less than that of my salad plate, I'll never know. The conversation turned to weight control, as it always does when women are eating out. Linda soon began her pep talk.

"Becky, you've got to start running. I feel so good about myself since I started jogging, it's unbelievable."

"Did you hear about the lady who ruined her knees while running?" I inquired. "They say she may never walk again."

Mimi appeared not to hear me and nodded her beautifully tanned and trimmed head in agreement with Linda. "It's given me self-confidence. A feeling of power," she insisted.

"Funny," I muttered, "I ran a block or two last week and could hardly get out of bed the next day."

Linda flexed a bicep and smiled. "We are woman, hear us roar!"

With so much energy surging in the atmosphere around me, I suddenly had the overpowering urge to take a nap. I am woman, hear me snore.

I did notice that Lori had been quiet during all the cheerleading, and though she is basically the size of a trim gnat, I knew she shared with me her dislike for the concept of habitual exercise. So when Linda complained that she hated to take off two weeks from her running schedule for a needed surgery, Lori leaned in my direction and covered her mouth with her napkin.

"I don't know about you," she whispered softly, "but I'd rather have the surgery." I couldn't have agreed more. However, I couldn't argue with the results. Linda and Mimi *are* stunning. And shouldn't Scott have a beautiful, thin, athletic, roaring wife, too? So, about a week ago, I started running.

On Day One my athletic son, Zeke, noticed my running form and passed the first several minutes of my warm-up time just trying to gain control of himself. So what if my shorts were held together by a bobby pin and kept popping open while my tanktop kept creeping up as I jogged. Big Deal. Somewhere around the bend of the first block, I began to hear the theme from *Chariots of Fire* playing in my head. I would press on toward the prize of my high calling.

This has been going on for about a week , and now that Scott and I are both officially athletes, it has opened up a whole new world for us as husband and wife. We've found another common ground—a mutual interest. Believe it or not, I am now actually running triathalons. Well, they are more like tri-atha-*lawns*. I run past at least three lawns before I collapse. While I lie on the asphalt gasping for air, Scott jogs in circles around me.

"Becky, get up! Come on, get up!" he gently coaches. "There's a car coming around the corner, and you're about to be road kill!"

To my amazement, Scott has recently taken up one of *my* favorite hobbies—reading. For years, he has considered a book to be the equivalent of a giant sleeping pill—a surefire cure for insomnia. Try as he might, he could never get past the first page before his chin drooped to his chest, his eyes slipped to half-mast, and his mouth fell open. When we were newlyweds, however, he loved for *me* to read to him. We had no television set, so we passed many an evening snuggled together under an afghan taking turns reading aloud from a gripping novel.

I've always been a read-aholic, an addiction Scott could never fully understand. I usually have at least three books going at once. A few weeks ago, I couldn't sleep, so I slipped out of bed at 2:00 A.M. and made a quick dash to an all-night superstore for a quick "fix." I picked out three paperbacks and as I was paying for my purchases, I realized the books sort of describe the three areas where my mind tends to dwell. I had chosen *In His Steps* (I truly do want to grow spiritually), *Seven Habits of Highly Effective People* (there's a highly effective person in me just waiting to get out, I hope), and the detective thriller, *Outsmarting the Female Fat Cell.* See what I mean?

I read anywhere—in the bathtub, in a hammock, in a lounge chair, in line at the grocery store, in the car waiting for a light to turn green. Sometimes, I even find my literary style strangely influenced by the great authors I have read in the past. (Oh, I would read books in a box. I would read them with a fox. In a house. In a tree. I do so love to read you see!)

I thought I knew my husband, but Scott has suddenly turned into Library Man. He turns off the television and actually reads—with his eyes open—for as much as an hour at a time. Suddenly we find ourselves silently reading our individual books together in bed, side by side, just like married people on old television shows. Granted, I'm reading romances, and he's reading cliff-hanger novels, but the important thing here is we've suddenly found another point of common interest. Seeing that common interests haven't been all that common in our relationship, the fact that we are now both athletes *and* avid readers is extremely exciting. We're beginning to blend!

When we stop to examine the families from which we sprang (sprung?), it's kind of a miracle that we have managed to get along as well as we have. Scott's parents hailed from a military background. Jim Freeman made sure his boys knew the value of hard work, and Scott is doing his best to pass that trait on to our children. Family vacations were most often filled with physical activity—camping, ski trips, and so forth. Not surprisingly, there are stoic, hard-working ancestors among the branches of Scott's family tree.

Scott tells me that having control of one's emotions was considered honorable, even practical, for the most part. So I think it's safe to say that Scott grew up in a mostly matter-of-fact, let's-get-to-work, no frills family environment, especially where his dad was concerned.

On the other hand, many of my ancestors might be best described as "Frills Are Us." Theatrical personalities flit through the branches of our tree. When we communicate praise, it's with effusive gushing. When we laugh, it's the belly-shaking, knee-slapping, tear-wiping sort. At the same time, we're a sensitive lot, so disappointments are accompanied by much throwing ourselves across the bed in heartrending sobs. Writers, persuasive lawyers, dancers, actors, and inventors roost among us. Affectionate, funny, dramatic, wordy—many of us (present company excluded, of course) are even considered by others to be a bit on the eccentric side.

Now, put those two backgrounds in the ol' marriage blender, and you can imagine what an "interesting" family Scott and I have managed to turn out. When our kids get hurt, Scott tells them things like, "Buck up! Keep a stiff upper lip, son!" At the same time, I'm likely to be luring them into my lap and to a rocking chair for a "huggy time," even if they're so big their feet drag the floor.

Obviously we bring diverse backdrops into the way we communicate with each other and the way we are raising our children. As a result we firmly believe our children will grow up to be nicely balanced. Or hopelessly confused.

But—are humans simply the sum total of genes and environments? Even as I describe Scott's and my families of origin, I realize that at best it is an oversimplification. Somewhere in Scott's family background, there must be some romantic genes floating around—because I see such sensitivity and desire for communication in my husband. And somewhere in my family background, there is also a level-headed, even somewhat driven, business sense I've been surprised to discover in my own seemingly scatterbrained personality. Both of us feel at times like strange dichotomies. Or maybe families and the people who make them up can't be pigeon-holed as easily as some psychologists might like to believe.

The other night Scott gave me a personality quiz he had already taken at work. By the time he had finished with me I was purple and blue. Seriously. Those are my two dominant personality colors, which Scott scientifically interpreted, using a crayon on the back of a scrap paper. He allowed as how I was trusting, spontaneous, rebellious, optimistic, imaginative, and manipulative. Surprise, surprise. Scott, in turn, was green and red. His dominant colors indicate he is competent and steady, logical and helpful, and excels in emergencies (my purple gives his red plenty of practice in this area). But it is important to note that neither of our personality types fell into just one hue. There's some green, red, purple, and blue in each of us, and even if the doses are minute—they are there.

Families and the people who inhabit them—rather than actually becoming a blender full of paint where all colors mix into one—are more like a swirling kaleidoscope. It's as if the Master Artist pauses at our personal canvas, dabs a little from the Palette of our Family Genes, and thoughtfully begins our portrait. But the miracle that brings each of us to life—what makes us uniquely who we are—comes from a magnificent array of colors known only to the Creator. These special colors we share with none of God's other children. They are ours alone.

In the hands of the Craftsman, we, our ancestors, our parents, our children, and the children that are to come will indeed share many shades and tones. And yet each of our works of art always stands alone, as divinely unique as He is uniquely divine. The wonderful part of this plan is that as we yield ourselves to the Master Designer—the portrait is always in progress—we are constantly growing and changing into new works of art.

When we come to the union of marriage we bring with us hues and tints from those whose loins we came and in whose homes we were raised. I know my mother's passion and my daddy's inquisitive nature pulse through my veins. Scott speaks with the quiet voice and gentle brown eyes so like his mother's and works with the same forceful energy of his father.

But the really great thing about joining with another person in the act of marriage—the thing that makes it such a mystery—is that for the first time in our lives we leave our father and our mother and we cleave to someone totally "other" than ourselves. Scott and I share no genetic material in common, but we marry the flavors of our souls and spirit—by choice—into a relationship that is as one-of-kind as the two people who form it. And when that marriage is aged and blended—not too much, but gently as with the slightest swirl of a spoon—mmmmm, it's refreshing!

For this cause shall a man leave his father and mother,
and shall be joined unto his wife,
and they two shall be one flesh.
This is a great mystery.

EPHESIANS 5:31–32, KJV
ॐ

Fly Me to My Mother's Nest, I'm One Sick Chick!

When I was a little girl, being sick, but not miserably so, was just about one of my favorite experiences. My mother turned into a vision of Florence Nightingale, reading stories, bringing chopped ice for me to chew and bed trays so pretty even dry toast and Jell-O looked like a gourmet treat. The highlight of the occasion was wearing Daddy's big soft yellow terry cloth robe. It was *almost* to die for.

If all of us kids happened to have a virus at the same time, we went into highly competitive theatrical performances, each one trying to outwrithe the others to secure the grand prize robe. As a matter of fact, as a child I was sure the title on the best-selling novel, *The Robe,* must have referred to the yellow terry cloth garment hanging in my daddy's closet. It still hangs in my parents' hall closet, next to my wedding dress. When I spied it during my last visit, sentimental memories of nausea and fever tugged at my heart.

You can just imagine my shock when I discovered Scott's family did not celebrate headaches, colds, *or* viruses. As a matter of fact, when someone in Scott's family got sick he was expected to stay in bed and REST until he was well! No sneaking off to the mall for chicken soup at the cafeteria. No TV, board games, and undivided attention over a mere sniffle.

The first year we were married, Scott was at a complete loss over what to do with me when I came down with a fever and sore throat. He had never witnessed anything quite like the scene that opened before him. He peeked into the bedroom where I lay, my eyes closed, moaning at appropriate intervals, my open hand flung delicately across my forehead.

"Um . . . how ya doin' in here?" he asked nervously, wondering how on earth to handle a new bride with a head cold who, for all appearances, seemed to be on her deathbed.

With Shakespearean skill I answered, "Forgive me if I my small griefs magnify, but mighten I bother you for a small glass of water and an aspirin before I fade away into that deep, dark night?"

"Huh?" Scott asked.

"Come closer, " I whispered until he bent down next to my fevered brow. Then I continued, "Take me home to Mother. Then go far, far away."

He did so and continued to resort to this escape hatch for the first few years of our marriage. Then Mother moved to Virginia, and we were stuck between a headache and a hard place. The inevitable happened, and I came down with an episode of the "vomitingmoblis." Amid loud clanging of pots and wide-eyed toddlers, Scott managed to prepare a bedtray for me. Never mind that it was a hamburger with a plateful of warm pork and beans mixed with mayonnaise and delivered on a cookie sheet—it was the thought that counted.

When I first came at Scott with a bedtray of cool wash cloths, thermometers, medicine, bland-but-beautiful food, a magazine, flowers, and a mint, he looked at me as if I were an alien life-form. I eventually realized that his plea, "Just leave me alone," truly meant, "Just leave him alone."

As the years passed, I became a little more stoic, and Scott gave nurturing his best shot. I came to accept that Scott truly preferred that I not fuss over him when he succumbed to illness.

So how have Scott and I handled the illnesses of our own children? It all hinges on whether we are discussing illness or accidents. At this writing, the kids and I are swimming down at the pier, and I have just taken a scientific sampling on this matter. The question I posed from under my sunshades was direct and simple.

"Which parent do you want around when you are sick?" Unanimously from under and above the water came the answer.

"You, Mom!"

Then I rephrased the question slightly. "Which parent do you want around when you've been hurt?"

The answer was just as forthright.

"Dad!"

Perhaps I should explain. When I hear a child screaming in pain as a result of injuring himself, my first reaction is to look around for any other adult or near-adult who can take over. I'm not proud of this, mind you, but I'm extremely queasy when it comes to the sight of blood.

If it turns out that I *must* be the one to come to the aid of the victim, I always follow the same first aid procedure. I arm myself with the biggest towel I can find and then walk backwards toward the injured party in order to avoid the sight of blood. Then I toss the towel over my shoulder toward the victim, like a bride throwing her bouquet, and instruct the child to cover the wound. Once "it" is disguised, I am better able to render aid and comfort, one small step at a time. My motto is, "What you can't see can't possibly hurt."

This method didn't work as well last fall when Zach abruptly yelped in pain and came running into the kitchen holding one limp hand in the other. I immediately turned my back, grabbed a large kitchen towel, shut my eyes, and threw it over my shoulder and in Zach's general direction. When I got up the nerve to peek, I saw that his hand was sufficiently intact, so I calmly walked over to him and applied pressure through the towel to his hand. He turned pale and screamed.

"Mom! Stop squeezing! It's not cut. It's broken!" A couple of X-rays and $400 later, I discovered his diagnosis was indeed correct. So I'm not a paramedic.

On another occasion, I had taken Zeke, Rachel Praise, and Gabriel with me to our local Cherry's Christian Bookstore. I led the troops toward the store, with Zeke bringing up the rear. As we were about to walk in the front door, I heard Zeke's voice behind me.

"Mom," he said, his voice sounding a bit worried, "I think I need to go the hospital or something."

Because he was so calm, there was no warning that I needed to shut my eyes. So I turned around, and there Zeke stood with his leg split down his shin bone from knee cap to ankle, the skin rolled back like a scroll, exposing the bone.

Fighting nausea, I hollered to the people inside the bookstore, "My son just cut himself really bad on a license plate or something! Does anybody here have anything to put on it to stop the bleeding?!"

I then ran to the van and grabbed what makeshift dressing I could find, surprising myself with my clear head. At the same time, three ladies exited the store, each carrying what they could contribute to the cause.

When I finally got my son into the doctor for stitches, the nurses were in stitches themselves. "Did you know," asked the head nurse, "that I pulled a roll of paper towels, a disposable diaper, a box of Kleenex, a T-shirt, a dish towel, and several grass clippings off your son's leg? What were you trying to do—*suffocate* the wound?"

I never claimed to be a rock in a crisis, but Scott, on the other hand, is. A couple of years ago, I was taking a night class, and on the night of my final exam, Scott was to come home to baby-sit the kids for me. He was late, and I was frantic that I was going to be late and flunk the class. When he pulled into the driveway, he tossed me the keys and said, "Go!" I was irritated, but I had to get on the road or miss the important test. When I got home from class that night, I casually asked Scott why he had been so late. I had assumed it had been the Dallas traffic, but his answer stunned me.

"Oh, I came upon an accident on the highway. There was a woman in a truck who needed a little help until the ambulance arrived. She had split open all of the skin on the top of her head, so I held her head in my lap while I applied pressure to her wound and talked to her until the emergency crew arrived." Mind you, he said this in the same manner he might say, "I had the Chinese buffet at Wing Wang's for lunch."

Of course, my husband may not be my first choice for a comfort provider when I'm not feeling quite up to par. However, if my head actually ever *does* come apart at the seams, Scott is definitely the man I want to be on hand.

The only thing worse than not being able to help your child who is in pain is getting tickled at the way he or she looks when they've received an injury of the minor variety. Has any other mom on the planet had a hard time suppressing a giggle when their child has some sort of not serious bug bite or a reaction to one—a reaction that inflates a facial feature way out of proportion to the rest of his or her face? The worst, of course, is the old "swelled upper lip problem" that leaves the child looking as if he belongs to parents by the name of Donald and Daisy.

My cousin, Jamie, recently called to tell me that her very sensitive child, Jacob, had the swollen lip affliction and that she had nearly bitten through her own lip trying desperately not to laugh at the way he looked. But then along comes Jacob's little sister, too young to know about such things as tact.

"Mommy!" she blurted out, "Jacob looks just like a duck, doesn't he?" Of course, Jamie was a goner. All the while she was comforting Jacob and heartily denying the obvious fact that he indeed looked very much like a mallard, she was laughing so hard the tears poured down her face.

Later that evening she found Jacob working quietly at his desk with pencil and paper, his upper lip still casting a remarkable shadow in the lamplight. Hoping they were friends again, Jamie asked pleasantly, "Whatcha doin', Jacob?" Without even glancing in her direction, Jacob continued writing.

"I'm making a list of all of the people who laughed at my lip today, and I'm starting with you," he answered. Jamie started to apologize all over again, but then Jacob's upper lip began to flap as he talked, and she had to run into the bathroom and lock herself in so he wouldn't see her losing it again. This is exactly the kind of situation that keeps getting Jamie and me knocked off the Mother of the Year nominee list time after time.

When my Zeke was about two his left ear was stung by either a bee or a high-octane mosquito. He was such a cute, skinny little guy to start with, but with his ear standing straight out from the side of his head, he looked exactly like Dopey, my favorite dwarf. We enjoyed him so much that way I almost hated to see the swelling go down.

My mother understands my predicament and sympathizes. She tells me that she had a terrible time when my brother David and I both had the mumps at the same time. I remember as if it were yesterday, seeing my jowls hanging down from my face as I stared at my five-year-old reflection in the mirror.

Mother had done her best to make me feel pretty by dotting my cheeks with her rouge and putting pink lipstick on my mouth. It was no use. I just looked like a very *feminine* Droopy Dawg, and David bore a remarkable resemblance to Mighty Mouse. When David's pain was most intense, he was comforted by the application of Band-Aids on each cheek.

Our favorite family fun comes after a trip to the dentist. If the doctor has numbed one of my children's lips, we all come down with a case of the giggles. (Sick humor?) Maybe it's just because we're hard up for good recreation, but watching the freshly released patient try to smile—or better yet, laugh—with half his or her mouth asleep is more fun than watching any slapstick comedy routine. If the anesthetized sibling is willing to try to sip a drink or slurp soup from a spoon for our amusement—well, let's just say it doesn't get much better than that when it comes to quality family entertainment.

Mother says I had my share of visits to the emergency room as a child for things like eating decorative rocks from the potted plants at restaurants. And I still remember the wild dash to the doctor to remove the raisin I had pushed up my nose. But one of the funniest episodes I remember with my own children started out to be rather scary.

One day when Gabriel was about two, he was having one of those "Too Quiet Times." When I finally located him, he was holding an empty bottle of his antihistamine/cough syrup. I didn't really think there had been enough medicine left in the bottle to do any damage, but the doctor advised me to go ahead and give Gabe some syrup of Ipecac just to be on the safe side.

As it turned out, Gabe *loved* the syrup, but he seemed to be especially delighted with the whole process of throwing up. Crazy as it sounds, I have witnesses who can attest to the fact that Gabe would throw up, then laugh with glee, throw up, laugh, and so on. It was all a festive occasion to him. He was far and away the happiest victim of induced vomiting I've ever seen—possibly the only one.

As I said earlier, Scott and I have come from very different backgrounds when it comes to handling sickness. The solution to this problem has come in the form of compromise. As with most things, we've drawn a few of the bedside manners and home remedies we like best from our families of origin and are settling into our own unique methods of coping in times of minor illness and accidents. I hardly ever even *think* about flying home to my mother during health crises anymore.

I'm coping so well in fact that I'm actually considering applying for certification to teach several health related seminars

I have developed all on my own. The medical community may never be quite the same again.

A merry heart doeth good like a medicine.

PROVERBS 17:22, KJV

∾

A Pair of Talking Mynah (League) Birds

News travels fast in our small town, and when word got out that I had coauthored a book about worms, my status immediately grew. As a matter of fact, I found myself proudly introduced in public places as "the author with *Worms*." Another friend came up with a promotion ploy—suggesting Mother and I wear buttons that read, "Ask us about our *Worms*."

With that sort of interest, invitations to speak began to pour in. OK, so I dropped a hint over the phone to the ladies' committee chairwoman from my church that I just might be available to speak at our annual Ladies' Class Christmas Coffee.

When I arrived at the home where the tea was to take place, it looked as if it belonged to Martha Stewart on one of her better Christmases. Elegant, it was, with a roaring fire in the huge stone fireplace, luxurious furniture covered in rich tapestries and the entire house accentuated with holly, ivy, lace, candles, flowers—the works.

By a great miracle, I had arrived early, and I soon saw that the hostesses were having trouble with the spout of a gorgeous silver coffee urn. It would not stop dripping. There it stood in the middle of the white damask cloth with two nicely burning votive candles on either side, its spout creating a puddle in a hastily placed crystal punch cup. I couldn't help thinking that perhaps the Spirit had prompted me to arrive early because He had foreseen my skills would be needed. Readers of our first book will already know that I have become somewhat of an expert on leaking things—appliances, car radiators, commodes, sewers. Why wouldn't these skills transfer to an elegant silver coffee urn?

I jiggled the spout in a more professional manner than the hostess had been jiggling it, and when the puddle continued to grow, I bent low and tried to peer up the spout itself. Clearly I was onto something. A *most* peculiar odor began to rise, followed by a puff of smoke wafting before my eyes. Suddenly the hostesses sprang at me from all directions, beating me about the head and shoulders with towels and tossing cups of water in my general direction. When I realized I had managed to ignite my hair in the votive candles beside the urn, I did exactly what I had taught my first graders to do in our Safety First Course: I stopped, dropped, and rolled all the way to an easy chair where the hostesses insisted I stay until it was time for me to speak.

"We don't want anything else to happen, Becky," they assured me, and I was touched by their concern for me.

My topic for the morning was "Taking Time to Wonder as You Wander Through the Season," and I'm sure the ladies were wondering why the hostess had included the fragrance of singed hair with the potpourri on her tables. Considering the elegance of the rest of her decorations, I expect we may have the seen the evolution of an entirely new Christmas fragrance. Watch for it next year. It transports one almost immediately to a stable.

I had planned to end my talk with a moving quote about the love of a father for his young son. At the peak of this tender, emotion-charged moment, the sterno heater on the buffet table suddenly ignited, shooting flames about two feet into the air. It created quite a stir, but our Christmas Coffee Women's Volunteer Fire Department leaped into action, beating the flames with dish towels, trying to subdue the inferno with crystal cups full of punch and coffee and, finally, extinguishing the persistent flames with an inverted fondue pot. When the hostesses looked in my direction, I was thankful I had been standing at least three yards from the table during the event.

Other than these two teensy little interruptions, I thought my first speaking engagement went pretty well. A few weeks later, both Mother and I were invited to speak at a mother/daughter banquet at a church in the pretty little East Texas town of Kilgore. On the drive down, I sat in the back seat enjoying the peace and quiet and wondering how Scott was faring back at the ranch with our four kiddos. Mother, however, had her mind on the upcoming speaking engagement.

"Don't you think we should do a little coordinating of what we might say? I have my speech all typed out," she informed me with satisfaction. "It's right here in this folder." She was holding onto it tightly.

"You wrote out every word?" I asked.

"Yes. I don't plan to read it, but I just feel more comfortable if I have the entire speech before me in black and white. The audience will hardly notice. Since you'll be speaking first, I'll just put it on the speaker's stand before the banquet starts, and it will be there when my turn comes." It seemed to me she was doing it the hard way, but I decided not to tell her so. I'm independent, but I'm not foolhardy.

When we arrived, Mother noticed that I had gotten ink from a ballpoint pen on my white blouse, dead center. I was also wearing a vest which I had left unbuttoned because it was too tight.

"Becky," Mother decided, "if you don't mind having your chest crushed I think we can button the vest over the stain. What do you think?" She decided she didn't really want to know what I thought and offered another suggestion. "Maybe you could make your speech while taking very shallow breaths?"

We decided to go with that plan, and then I glanced with something akin to envy at Mother's flowingly comfortable and spotless hot pink knit dress with the lavender bow at the waist—and was absolutely delighted to discover a moist, half-consumed breath mint nestling in the bow just about even with her belly button.

"Mother!" I hissed, "You've got to stop drooling and learn to hang on to your breath mint if you want to make any kind of impression at this nice banquet!" She was unperturbed. Raising the one eyebrow she raises so well, she gave me a nonchalant smile, peeled the mint off her lavender belt, and popped it back into her mouth.

As soon as we arrived at the church, Mother hurried up front to the speaker's stand to place her folder of notes just so.

I spoke first and had a number of books from which I read a number of touching quotes and excerpts, but at the end of my speech, I had a little difficulty getting it all together. I had a large stack of now katywhompus papers, books, and visual aids to take with me back to my seat. I began to feel as though I were packing for a trip through the Yukon in front of an audience that seemed to be growing restless. Before it was all together, I got my wrist tangled in an electric cord and dropped one book (a hardback) on my foot, but I left the podium clean as a whistle.

Mother stepped to the podium, cleared her throat, and turned panic-stricken eyes in my direction. "Ahem," she said. "Becky, dear, do you have my notes?"

I promise, I *didn't* do it on purpose! By that point in the afternoon, I'm sure Mother would have gladly rented me a private nest in someone else's family tree.

Afterwards, the ladies and their daughters were polite and kind, but no one gushed. It should be noted that Mother and I require copious gushing. However, Daddy came through for us, doing the best job of gushing a man can do. During the two-hour drive back home, he stopped at a nearby country cafe to treat us to a relaxing dinner. Since the cafe was about the only one in this neck of the woods, and since it was Saturday night, a stream of harried waitresses carrying plate after plate of chicken fried steak and cream gravy burst through the swinging doors from the kitchen. Forty-five minutes later, none of them had been ours, so I asked Mother if she had any of her breath mints left I could munch on.

After a few mints, I excused myself to go to the ladies' room, which seemed to be occupied. At least, I tugged on the door and it didn't open, so I leaned against the wall and waited. Soon a cute little cowgirl, about eighteen, joined me in my vigil. I said "Hi," but she didn't seem to want to chat, so we lapsed into silence. And lapsed. And lapsed. Finally, an idea occurred to me.

"Wouldn't it be funny if no one was in there? You and me standing out here, twiddling our thumbs, waiting all this time? Wouldn't that be funny?" With that, the cowgirl reached out, took firm hold of the doorknob, gave it a twist and—sha-zam! the door fell open. She turned hard eyes upon me.

"How 'bout that?" I giggled. "Not a soul in there after all."

With an expression of contempt, she said, "*You goon!*" and stomped into the restroom, closing the door in my face. And I had been in line first! Well, I did what any self-assured, assertive woman of the nineties would do. I went back to my parents' table and told my daddy on her. Daddy said I most certainly was not a goon and would have gone to defend my honor had I not held him back. I felt a little better, but I couldn't help wondering if a brief history of my speaking career might be summed up in one simple sentence: Hair today, goon tomorrow.

Wherefore, my beloved brethren, let every man be swift to hear, slow to speak.

JAMES 1:19, KJV

~

Shall We Hatch Young, or Fly South for the Winter?

I often wondered why our best "couple" friends, Dean and Heather, continued to invite us over. Their peaceful home was uninhabited by small children, and their lifestyle was one of freedom and serenity. For six years, I waddled into their immaculate home, eternally pregnant and holding at least one toddler and/or rambunctious child by the hand. Each year, they had definitely decided not to have children, and that was semifinal.

Yet Heather seemed genuinely intrigued with us. She always plied me with questions, like a reporter gathering information from some lost Aborigine tribe. She seemed to find it absolutely fascinating that I could survive four small children amid a life of total disarray and still smile occasionally—even *frequently.*

They were the perfect modern host and hostess, cooking side by side and serving our scrumptious meals together. But once our brood dropped off to sleep, Scott and I reveled in the soft music drifting from the stereo in the background and in the uninterrupted and oh-so-adult conversation. Strangely, it often drifted to the Big Question.

"What's a good reason and when is a good time, if ever, to have a baby?" I'll have to admit, it wasn't easy to come up with a quick answer. And how could I risk ruffling such neatly placed feathers? Dean had a teenage son by a previous marriage whom he adored, and his fatherly instincts seemed to have been completely satisfied. Heather had a great job with an airline, and they frequently jetted off to New York or California and sometimes even Europe as nonchalantly as other young couples go out for dinner and a movie. Both were pursuing higher degrees. As precious as my children were to me, I thought about what a child would do to Dean and Heather's lives—and not just big adjustments, either. What about the everyday irritations? It was in this arena that I found I needed all my coping skills.

First of all, children can be as hard on the body of an unsuspecting parent as lethal weapons. Numerous times I have bent to greet one of my children with a loving embrace, only to have the child leap to greet me at the same instant, thereby smearing my shnoz and kisser all over my face with the top of his or her bony little head. The pain is searing and there's no workmen's comp to fall back on. Come to think of it, I don't even get the afternoon off. This is not a job for couples with slow reflexes.

It's probably not the *best* job for people who like to live in perfectly clean houses, either. I truly believe that all mothers have the potential to keep immaculate houses, even though it has been said that only dull women have immaculate houses. The problem surfaces when one puts *children* into the house. Not only will the house receive immeasurable wear and tear, I've come to the conclusion that most little boys, and a few little girls, can destroy an anvil, given the time and opportunity.

When a mother discovers the anvil has indeed been destroyed, she eventually learns—particularly if she has more than one child—that she must acquire detective skills that would qualify her for the staff at Scotland Yard in order to determine who dunnit. Almost always, it is Nobody. Therefore, we soon learn not to ask, "Zachary, did you tear up the anvil?" Of course he didn't. Neither did Ezekiel. *Nobody* did it. A far better way to get to the bottom of things is to ask, "Zach, *when* did you tear up the anvil?" If Zachary *is* the culprit, he assumes that you know, and the jig is up. If he is not guilty, his denial will be so genuinely indignant that you can then logically deduce that the culprit is Zeke. Voilà! This is not a job for the slow-witted.

Being a parent can be hard on the reputation as well. I know perfectly good mothers who have tarnished reputations simply because they feel they must allow their toddlers to learn to choose their own clothes and to dress themselves. If a child learning to put his shoes on has a 50 percent chance of getting them on the right feet, how can he miss 100 percent of the time? And getting them off his feet and on the right ones is like wrestling an alligator. How many participatory managers would have the patience to put up with *that*? Parenting is not a job for couples who want a low-maintenance lifestyle.

Having children can also be hard on your health. Mother assures me that once our children are gone from home, Scott and I will no longer be subject to the twenty-four-hour virus that sweeps through our home on a bimonthly basis (or so it seems), leaving each family member in turn, green and heaving, on the bathroom floor. Those are the times when I, too, daydream about putting on a navy blue suit, white blouse, and red scarf and heading for the office.

Considering all the things children can do to age parents virtually overnight, why do people in their right minds continue to make careers out of raising them? I understand that some home economics classes are giving teenagers a glimpse of the responsibility that goes with having a child. The students are given an egg which they are to keep with them constantly for several days, tending to the egg as if it were their child. I suppose this can seem like a novelty for an hour or so, but it probably gets to be a drag before the assignment is over, just as it sometimes gets to be a drag for parents not even to be able to run to the grocery store for a loaf of bread without making provision for the baby's care. But somehow, when it's *your* baby, it never enters your mind to drop it on its head or wish you didn't have it.

Trying to explain what it is like to love your own baby (even when he's spitting up on your silk blouse) to a childless couple is like trying to describe a rainbow to a blind man. Oh, there are comparisons and metaphors, but when it comes right down to brass tacks, there are some things that must be *experienced* to be understood. There are no virtual reality computer babies, yet.

Before my sister, Rachel, and her husband, Gilley, (that's short for Scott St. John Gilbert III) decided to have a child, they approached it with their usual careful deliberation and profound common sense. Their hesitation may have been related to the fact that she had been present at the home birth of our third child—the one when the midwife didn't get there in time. It may have had something to do with the time she visited our little family (six in number by then) just after we moved into our 865-square-foot lake cabin. I think she may have been looking for reassurance when she wrote Mother and asked her if, in her opinion, having children in today's world was really a smart idea. This was Mother's reply:

Dearest Rachel and Gilley,

I can understand the logic in today's world of choosing not to have children. It is an awesome responsibility—to bring a person into being who will be a part of our lives as long as we live, and sometimes that means an unending responsibility. Children can bring us a good deal of pain, some more than others. But they can also bring unmatched joy. What more worthwhile thing could we do with our lives than to shape and mold another human being?

It is certainly true that life can be so much more orderly and under control when only adults are involved. Once you children were raised, Daddy and I settled quickly into our comfortable, clean, quiet, unencumbered life. But—I wonder if we would enjoy it as much if we had always had it. Bearing and raising children is a sustained, intense course in learning to give—of every part of our being and life. Contrary to what you may be hearing today, I've found that the less self-centered we are, the happier our lives seem to be.

The intensity of love we feel for our offspring is unique, more gripping than any other emotion we experience, I think. But what if we should lose that child to an accident or an illness? The agony would be indescribable. Why not avoid the potential for pain? But the same thing is true, perhaps in lesser degree, about any one we love, and not many of us are willing to live life without love in order to avoid being hurt.

I fear that people who make the decision not to have children when they are young have no idea what it will be like to be middle-aged and finally, old. When your Nonnie was widowed and began to age at about sixty-five, her children became her whole world, her emotional support, and often, her providers. Then, when she became helpless, I shudder to think what would have been her lot at the nursing home if I had not been there most every day to check on her. I've seen the loneliness and desolation of the elderly who have no one to look after them. What happens to childless people? Perhaps this isn't a good reason to bring a child into the world, but it certainly is a fringe benefit.

On the other hand, it may be that this is not a good time in history to bring children into the world. Who knows the future? It is certainly something to consider at any time, I suppose, and only the couple involved can make the decision. Just getting out of bed in the morning takes a lot of faith these days, but it *is* an adventure.

In case you and Gilley may be considering the option of not having children, Daddy and I want you to know it will be fine with us. We will not think less of you at all and will certainly respect your judgment. And we will enjoy the times we can share with you as four adults that we can't really have with Becky and Scott for a few years yet. Their lives are different, and we enjoy different things with them. And you and Becky are so very different. I have loved sharing your very different lives and activities.

I am intensely grateful to have had the precious children we had and to have been financially able to be at home with you as you grew up. I realize more every day how much harder it is for this generation to choose that life. I think if I knew for certain I would have to work all the time I was raising children, I might give it more serious thought before embarking on the adventure.

I will add this one last thought, and then close. Having children is like eating regular meals—wonderfully satisfying, but oh, so *daily*. On the other hand, having grandchildren is like having a hot fudge sundae when you haven't had sugar for a week! It's one of life's nicest surprises, one I didn't give much thought to until it happened to me. I can't imagine having missed it!

Bushels of love,
Mom

Mother was called to Virginia within the year to look after her new grandson, Trevor, and two years later we got this letter from my sister:

I'm tired! But mostly we are enjoying Trevor so much. He's sweet and bright and *loves a good time.* (And we wondered why he didn't want to sleep when he was a newborn!)

Bright Eyes has remained true to his birth nature. What a tremendous blessing he is. If (God forbid) he were gone tomorrow, I would still feel tremendously blessed to have known him. That's not meant to be morbid—just a statement of gratitude that God has entrusted him to us at all.

And Dean and Heather? Well, Dean is forty now. His hair is thinning just a tad and turning a distinguished shade of gray. Our friendship has only grown deeper over the years. Scott often speaks of Dean's ability to make others feel completely loved and accepted. When Dean completed his doctoral program this winter, we celebrated with them over pizza and cokes. Heather is just finishing her master's degree. Lest you think they have become all work and no play, they've also invited us to share a luxury condo in Florida on two separate occasions, and we are looking forward to doing it again this summer. It's great to have friends who are footloose and fancy free.

Well, sort of. Did I also mention that joining us last year on the Florida vacation was their tiny one-year-old daughter, Nicole, who has the biggest, bluest eyes I've ever seen? And did I tell you about sharing her parents' excitement as they watched her first reaction to the waves and salt and sand? Or about how Dean carries her everywhere in his backpack while Heather soaks up every sweet new word Nicole says with the delight only a mother of a toddler can experience?

Oh, yes. And I should also mention that Dean and Heather loved being parents so much that they decided to expand again. Their question, "What is one good reason to have a baby?" appeared to have changed dramatically with the reality of a child looking up at them from their arms. As I watched our two friends fall in love with their daughter, the haunting question seemed now to be replaced by an unspoken conclusion, "Who needs a reason?" So this summer Nicole will be accompanied to Florida by her new baby brother.

It was important to Dean and Heather that their new son carry a special name—the name of someone they loved and admired—a good and loyal friend. On the day the new baby was born, Dean called to tell us the name they had chosen for their newborn son. He will be called—Scott. On hearing the good news, my husband's eyes shone with pleasure all day.

On a recent visit to our house, we watched Dean and Heather unpack diapers and baby food and strollers and playpens and pacifiers and baby wipes from their family car, while Scott and I told them about the first-ever real vacation we are planning alone together, jetting away for four days in Colorado. The irony is not lost on us all, and the four of us smile and wonder at the reversals that have taken place in our lives. Funny, they don't seem to envy us our trip. I was relieved and pleased to see that Heather had happily discovered the secret of nesting mothers the world over.

Sure, kids can be a real pain. But during our visit, as Heather sat rocking Baby Scott while Nicole laughed and played with my children nearby, she smiled and her voice grew tender.

"Becky, thanks for encouraging me to do this. I'm so glad I didn't miss getting to be a mother."

There are some things in life—like watching a jet-setting, career-oriented friend turn into mother hen mush—you just have to *experience.*

Behold, children are a gift of the Lord; the fruit of the womb is a reward.

PSALM 127:3, NASB
୶

The Arnold Branch

Measuring Up
to a Rare Bird

As a new bride, I wrote a letter to our local newspaper to nom-
inate my dad, George Arnold, as "Father of the Year."
Among other things I wrote, "Daddy is the tenderest, most
loving man I know. . . . He never leaves for work without kissing
mother good-bye and he greets her with a warm hug when he
comes home. Every day of my life he told me he loved me and
that all of us children were precious to him. . . . My father is the
wisest man I know. . . . He has a living, vital relationship with
the Lord and has encouraged each of us in our Christian walk.
Daddy has a wonderful sense of humor," etc. It was quite a
tribute, but how would *you* have liked to have been the new
son-in-law?

Now, Scott loves my father (It can't be helped!) and considers
him one of his dearest friends, but it drove him nuts trying to
measure up to the standard of the father-in-law he sometimes
lovingly refers to as "St. George." How could anyone compete
with this gentle Big Bird of the Arnold family nest?

A couple of years ago when our family was on vacation at
Holly Lake in our beloved East Texas, I sat on the deck of our

rented condo with my husband, Scott; my brother, David and his wife, Barb; and my sister, Rachel and her husband, Gilley.

We could see Daddy several yards away down on the dock with his grandkids and knew he would be patiently putting worms on hooks for Gabriel, our seven-year-old budding fisherman. He would also have plenty of lines to untangle for Rachel Praise, our only female child, a halfhearted fisherwoman at best. If our preteen sons, Zach and Zeke, had a problem it would probably be the hardest of all to solve—retrieving expensive lures from the branches of tall trees. All of these chores Daddy would have to manage while trying to make sure David's little Tyler didn't fall in the water. Naturally enough, our conversation on the deck turned to St. George the Divine.

My memory drifted to the time when our family had just discovered this pine-covered paradise at Holly Lake, and if I squinted just right in the evening sun, Daddy's silver streaked hair looked almost 1969 black again. The voices of my own children faded to the long-ago sounds of me, David, and Rachel teasing and fussing and vying for Daddy's attention.

As I watched the fuzzy eventide scene, with thoughts drifting from Now to Then and back again, I was suddenly pulled from my reverie by David's manly chuckle.

"Hey, Rachel, remember that time you thought you had a huge bass and pulled your pole so hard you brought up about a gallon of seaweed? It hit Dad right upside the head! He turned real slow toward us, dead pan, with his head covered with green gook. Man, I thought I'd lose it!"

"Yeah, well," Rachel responded, deciding quickly that the best defense would be a good offense. "Don't forget the night Dad took you fishing fifty miles out in the country. As I recall, you topped off the end of a long day in the hot sun by dropping the car keys in the lake." David grinned, bit off a piece of fishing line, and went back to tying a lure, but Barb definitely wanted to pursue that topic.

"What did George say when David did *that?*" she asked.

"Oh," Rachel laughed, "I think he said something like, 'Aw . . . son, I can't believe you did that. I just *told* you to be careful when I handed them to you! Remember?' And that was the extent of the bawling out. Dad telephoned Mom from a marina, and she somehow managed to find us in the dark and bring an extra set of keys. By the time she got there, Dad was laughing about it and even had David tickled. He's got the patience of a . . . ."

"Saint?" Scott asked, throwing a "See what I'm up against?" look in my direction.

"Yeah," I laughed, determined to give Scott a more balanced view of my dad. "Sure, he's unique. But *nobody's* perfect!"

The faces staring back at me looked unconvinced.

"Well, OK, let's think. He must have a fault. . . . I know! He *hated* working on cars. I once heard him say 'darn' when the hood slammed down on his head."

"Good try," Rachel said, "but even though he hated it, after David and I both got our driver's licenses, he spent most of his Saturdays keeping three used cars running."

"Touché," I admitted. "File that under *self-sacrificing:* 'Looking out for the needs of others.'"

"OK, guys," interrupted Rachel's husband, Gilley. "He's *gotta* have some faults."

Scott reached over to pat the greenhorn son-in-law on the back. "Listen, Gilley, I've been at this son-in-law business a few years now, and I'll just save you some time here by asking a few questions: Have you ever seen George mad? Grouchy? Worried? In a hurry?"

Gilley thought over each question and then shook his head in amazement. "Come to think of it, I've never even seen him in an outfit that wasn't completely color coordinated."

I scratched my head. "He must have *some* sort of flaw. I *know* he does . . . ."

"Bound to," David agreed.

"Let me think a minute . . . ," said Rachel.

Just then Mother came out of the house to join us, iced tea in hand. "OK, Mom," Rachel challenged, "tell us some of Dad's faults! Don't hold anything back. We are all adults now. No use shielding us from the truth. We can take whatever it is."

Mother frowned, turned her chaise lounge away from the sun, pulled up a table for her tea, and stretched out. We could all see that she was thinking hard, and the silence hung heavy as we waited with great expectation for our father's darkest secrets to be revealed. Just as I was about to nod off, she spoke hesitantly.

"Well, . . . he *is* a slow eater."

I feigned a heartbreaking sob. "Oh, Mother! You've absolutely ruined our image of Daddy. How could we ever love him now, after such a horrifying confession!"

"I guess that's not too hard to live with," she conceded. "I've gotten a lot of mending done over the years waiting for him to finish his meals."

"What's 'mending'?" Scott asked, before I could slap my hand across his mouth. Suddenly, it was I who was in the "let's compare" hot seat. This same sort of question had come up before over another activity that Mother continued to insist on performing. "Dusting," I believe was the antiquated term she used. But I was ready this time with a life-saving definition for "mending."

"Scott, honey," I said with a great deal of equanimity, "mending was a quaint old-fashioned form of entertainment for premodern woman—before the invention of television. And the wheel." Then I quickly steered the conversation back to Mother. "Think hard, Woman!"

"There *is* one other thing that comes to mind," she said thoughtfully. "He never can *find* anything, even when I tell him exactly where it is. For years, no matter what he was looking for, he would go to the cabinet I described, open it, and stand there gazing into it."

"No!" we all gasped simultaneously.

"Yes!" Mother was hot on the trail now, thinking she'd really uncovered a dastardly habit. "'It's not here!' he would say. He *always* said, 'It's not here!' and then I would have to stop what I was doing and go stand beside him, reach into the cabinet and hand him the item. Then he would say, 'Oh.'"

"How did you ever cope?" Rachel exclaimed in exaggerated shock. "Did you think of divorce?"

"I finally taught him to say, 'I don't see it' instead of, 'It's not here!' and our relationship was saved." By this time, Mother was visibly worn with the trauma of reliving her nightmare. Barb was not impressed.

"Is that *it?!* " she asked. "That's his *one fault?*"

Mom wiped the perspiration off her forehead. She was really wracking her brain now. "Well, I guess by today's standards, I have spoiled him pretty badly. I *do* cut his hair, lay out his clothes every morning, and fix his cereal.

(*Oh, mother, please,* I thought. *Impressionable young husbands are listening to this.*)

"I even lay out his vitamins and fill a glass with water and leave it with them on the counter. I really fouled him up not long ago, though. I forgot to put his water glass out. He came into the kitchen, looked at his vitamins, and then looked at me in genuine puzzlement as if he didn't quite know what to do.

"'Where's my water?' he asked. I couldn't believe it!"

"'I keep it in the hydrant!' I told him, my voice dripping sarcasm."

That's tellin' him, Mother, I thought. *Mark up one point for the independent little woman!*

"Well," said Barb, "what did George say to that?"

Mother looked sheepish for a minute and then answered quietly, "I sort of forgot what he said after he laughed and laughed and then grabbed me around the waist and kissed me and told me how funny I was."

Scott, David, and Gilley gagged in unison. Rachel, Barb, and I were just happy to be off the "dusting" and "mending" topic, not to mention being let off the hair-cutting, clothes-laying-out, and cereal-pouring hooks.

Later that evening, as Scott and I were lying in bed, we came to some important conclusions. Daddy may be altogether without defect, at least to the naked human eye; Mother may be Susie Homemaker/ June Cleaver/ Julia Child rolled up in one. They may be so in love that it drips maple syrup around their house instead of raindrops. And we couldn't be happier for them.

But here in *our* relationship, in our home, in our lifestyle, we operate a little differently. First of all, we have finally admitted it—I don't do mornings. If someone handed me a bowl of prepoured cereal, odds are I couldn't accurately hit the bowl with the milk before 10:00 A.M. Scott has spent eighteen years waiting in vain for me to pop up some morning, like a toaster pastry, singing "Oh, What a Beautiful Morning" as I scramble farm-fresh eggs and country sausage with biscuits and cream gravy on the side. The truth of the matter is, he enjoys having his morning coffee alone in peace and quiet anyway. And, alas, my husband may never know a mended sock or a dusted shelf, which—come to think of it—he probably would enjoy.

On the other hand, Scott has been known to get rather testy, even angry and stubborn and moody on occasion. Furthermore, unless he's heading for the office, he can be a walking "fashion disastuh," as my friend from New Jersey says. I never know what time he is coming home in the evenings (he travels a lot), but you can bet it will be just after I've cleaned the kitchen and put supper completely away for the night. And though he is a romantic at heart and can be very tender, he doesn't effuse constant admiration of my every waking move, which has been a real letdown for me. I would really like constant admiration for my every waking move.

But—we love each other deeply. We've been best friends since we were fifteen and sixteen years old. We've gone through some rough times, but we like who we are as a couple. We like "us," warts and weirdness and wrinkles and all.

So we've made a deal. No more comparisons to my parents. No more subtle hints for spousal improvement. And we've actually found that as we accept each other and my parents, appreciating but not coveting the differences, we're enjoying each other's company more than ever before. It basically comes down to the old formula: I'm OK, you're OK, Mother's OK, and Daddy's—almost perfect. Evidently all three of his children had momentarily blanked out what it was like to take a cross-country automobile tour with St. George.

Each one should test his own actions.
Then he can take pride in himself,
without comparing himself to somebody else.

GALATIANS 6:4, NIV

I'm Just a Bird
in a Gilded Wagon

Recently my friend—let's just call her, "Please Don't Use My Name, My Mother Would Have a Fit"—called and asked me to shoot her in the foot if it ever crossed her mind to take a vacation with her parents again. "How I have managed to tie my own shoes, the strings unbleached and unstarched as they are, my mother will never know. . . ."

Please Don't Use My Name's call threw me into a spell of reverie, recalling a trip that I, an adult of fairly sound mind, took with my own fairly functional parents. Also accompanying us were Zach and Zeke, aged four and three, and Rachel Praise, my teething baby daughter. All three were, unfortunately, complete foreigners to the concept of "sit still." Scott, to his everlasting gratitude, was unable to join us for the voyage east.

By the time we reached our destination—my parent's home in Virginia, some fifteen hundred miles away—all of the adults on board were suffering from various degrees of dementia. I, in a delirious moment at a mealtime break, prayed fervently that the prizes in my sons' Kiddie Burger Boxes might be child-sized straight jackets and duct tape.

Another thing I had forgotten about car trips with my father was that this easygoing laid-back, "Happy Days" man would undergo an amazing transformation once we were on the road.

St. George the Divine would suddenly become Trail Boss of the Covered [station] Wagon, determined to get the herd to the railhead before winter snows set in. When the need for a treat or a comfort station became acute, we kids knew to watch for a gas station or cafe which would be on the "right" side of the freeway. It was as if he had never learned to use freeway crossover bridges or turn arounds. As we dug into stale crackers and peanut butter rations from the backseat, I began to wonder if it was my father who coined the term, "Meals on Wheels."

When this memory of my father, long submerged in the dark recesses of my childhood mind, sprang forth, I began to plan ahead. I positioned the kids with their noses pressed to the right-hand windows, training them to yell, "I see one, Grandpa George!" with split-second timing. But we were no match for Daddy's quick-draw excuses.

"Sorry, little hombres," Daddy would apologize faster than a speeding silver bullet, "can't get there from here!"

"But, Daddy!" I wailed after watching gas station after cafe whiz by. Eventually, I was forced to accept the Law of the New Concrete Frontier: Every gas station and cafe in America is built on the wrong side of the road.

So you can understand my deep sense of gratitude and relief when we circled the wagon and stopped for a rest at a shopping center in Staunton, Virginia. We came close to experiencing our first stampede as we elbowed each other out of the way to get inside to wide open air-conditioned SPACE! There we bought lunch, treats, and diapers, and just generally let the kids loose on the unsuspecting mall.

Once Cowboy Daddy rounded us back into the wagon amid shouts of "Head 'em up. Move 'em out!" Mother and I each tried to persuade him to let one of us drive for a while. If only he would have allowed one of us to escape the back recesses of the station wagon where babies cried and pooped and whined and wrestled, it would have been a respite and a privilege. When Daddy refused to let go of the reins, mother and I discussed forming a two-woman posse to calf rope him. We'd make him *think* "Rawhide" . . . .

Once we had hit the unlonesome trail again—wonder of wonders—all three kids dropped off to sleep—simultaneously! I took the opportunity to scrunch down in the back seat, propped up my bare feet between the heads of Mother and Daddy sitting up front, and prepared to join my Winkin', Blinkin,' and Nod in Slumberland.

I finally relaxed, but sleep didn't come as quickly as I had hoped. I rested by closing one eye and squinting at my father through the opening between my left big toe and the one next to it. I tried to imagine him as Mother had once described him in his heyday—a "Fonzie" of the fifties. Now, with the passage of time, he looked remarkably like Texas Senator Phil Gramm.

Through the opening between the toes on my right foot, my mother—the formerly brown-haired teeny bopper from Sweetwater High's Class of '55—now resembled another of Texas' senators—silver-haired Kay Bailey Hutchison. Imagine what kind of scandal a bloodthirsty reporter could stir up if he were to spot Mother and Daddy, gazing into each other's eyes and cooing in some candlelit restaurant, mistaking them for their political lookalikes. I might add that gazing and cooing was standard fare with most meals my parents shared, whether it took place in a fancy restaurant or the bill of fare happened to be hot dogs with pork and beans served on a paper plate.

Just as I was about to doze off, Rachel Praise stirred, and I detected a tell-tale odor rising. I looked on the floor of the car for the new sack of diapers I had bought at the shopping center. They were not there. Fighting panic, I began to paw under mounds of toys, pillows, suitcases, and blankets. It was no use.

"Whoa, Daddy! Stop the car!" I yelped. "I think I left the diapers on the top of the car when we were at the mall!"

Daddy reluctantly slowed the station wagon at the next turn-around (Aha! He *did* know how to do it!). Surely enough the diapers had apparently ridden shotgun on top of the wagon for a couple of miles out of Staunton before blowing off and landing on the side of the road. Can't you just hear the conversation in the car behind us?

"Oh, land's sake, Henry, duck! We're about to be flattened by industrial-sized Huggies!"

"You don't reckon' they're loaded, do ya, Ethel?"

To my enormous relief, we spotted the diapers by the side of the road *only* twenty miles back. I was delighted to see the diapers, but not delighted that we were going to have to redo those miles with the pleasure of wide-awake company. Daddy managed to stay John-Wayne cool, while Mother did what mothers do to make everybody feel better. She began a "Did I ever tell you about the time . . . " story guaranteed to make me appear to have the intelligence of a neurosurgeon compared to *her* at my age.

"If you think," she began, "that allowing your father to drive down the highway with a bag of diapers the size of a small glacier on top of his car is embarrassing *(OK, Mom, cut to the chase)*, wait until I tell you about the time we took our first trip with Grandmother and Grandaddy Arnold. Right after we were married, we drove with them from Sweetwater, in West Texas, all the way to the Gulf Coast to visit relatives, which was about the only kind of vacation most people took back in those days.

"In late May the weather in Texas is already too hot for comfort. It was then I learned quickly that your grandmother, Margaret, had absolute, unquestioned control over the air-conditioning button. At the time I had very little understanding of menopausal ladies, and I felt that the rest of us were entitled to some opinion on the temperature once in a while. It might have helped if she had said something like, 'It seems warm to me. Is anybody else, perhaps, a bit warm, too?' But no, it was always a sudden announcement which could not be denied.

"'It's *Hot!!*' And with a quick flick of her tiny hand the car became a subzero freezer on wheels.

"One of the things I *did* appreciate about her was that every two hours she expected to stop for pie and coffee." (*Oh, Mother, isn't it a bit cruel to mention stopping for pie and coffee while we are forced to remain in this vehicle, living on beef jerky and cold water biscuits from breakfast to lunch?*) Undaunted by the licking of my lips, she continued.

"Stopping so often was a little hard on your grandad whose nickname was 'Speedy' *(I believe I'm familiar with his son, Breakneck),* but it suited me. It gave me a chance to thaw out.

"We were facing a nine-hour drive, and after five hours or so, Grandaddy Arnold let your daddy drive. When he pulled to the side of the road to change drivers, I got out of the back seat, intending to sit beside your daddy in the front. My new father-in-law frowned.

"'Ruth Ann, George needs to keep his mind on his driving,' he warned.

"'I promise I won't bother him,' I said, and I thought I did rather well for several miles. But we *were* nineteen and had a lot to talk about, and most of it was funny, so there was perhaps a bit more giggling than appropriate going on. To pass the time, I measured my hand against his to see how much bigger it was and found it was not a lot. His hair seemed a little out of place, so I combed it for a few miles, which helped pass the time, but I could hear my father-in-law's teeth occasionally clacking.

"'George!' he would frequently bark, 'watch what you're doing!' And for a few miles, you could actually see daylight between us. Then my neck got tired, and Daddy's shoulder made such a nice cushion. That put my mouth close to his ear and it just begged to be nibbled. The next thing I knew, I found myself in the back seat next to my new mother-in-law with my new father-in-law sitting where I had been beside my new husband.

"I wanted to object, but at the time, my feelings toward Lloyd Arnold bordered on pure awe. I was from one of the poorest families in our small town, and though he was only a middle manager, he wore white shirts, a suit most of the time—and a dress hat when he went out! My daddy was a carpenter who wore long handles under his khaki work clothes. When he dressed up to walk to town to buy the daily paper—we didn't own a family car—he too wore a dress hat—and then buttoned the top button of the khaki shirt, minus of course, a tie. Heavy work boots completed his decked-out, go-to-town ensemble.

"I'm sure you remember Grandaddy Arnold as always spit spot immaculate—just as he still is. He never had a spare pound on his body, and he wore his thinning brown hair brushed straight back from his forehead. His nose has always been impressive, I guess to match the ears. As a fairly young man, he had cheerfully had his bad teeth pulled, but the dentures never fit very well. But like every other unpleasant and/or unexpected event in his life, he simply rattled the change in his pocket, whistled a tune, and got on with the show.

"When he was nervous or irritable, he made a clacking sound with the teeth in a way I thought was fascinating. In all the years I knew him he never referred to me as 'Ruthie,' though almost everyone else did. I was always, 'Ruth Ann,' but I knew it had more to do with his no-frills personality than with liking me.

"He was typical of the dads of that era—physically present with his family, caring in the crises, but not terribly communicative, especially about his faith. But his children knew they could count on him, and all three loved and respected him.

"As for Margaret, this was the first time I realized that no thought, however fleeting or insignificant, ever passed through her mind without being verbalized. Of course, I was young and self-centered, so the rest of the trip was one of the longest I ever remember taking. I was more than delighted to arrive at the coast and to meet all my other new relatives. I hoped beyond hope they were the strong, *silent* type. We spent the next day enjoying the cool sea breeze, and I felt that the whole world must surely be revolving around the newlyweds.

"The Arnolds are a table game family, and we kept a constant game of forty-two going on the screened porch. This was one of my favorite things about my new family, and we had a grand rivalry, a foretaste of many happy hours I would spend with my in-laws playing forty-two.

"The next day we loaded the car to drive in to Houston to meet more relatives, planning to stay a few days there before driving back to West Texas. As I recall, it was a fifty-mile drive and the air conditioning in the car played out about ten miles down the road, so you can imagine how many times your Grandmother Arnold let us know it was *Hot!* The heat did not, however, dampen her enthusiasm for describing every wild flower growing along the road in minute detail. It was a fifty-mile drive that seemed more like a hundred. Just as we pulled into the drive at Great-Grandmother's apartment, I realized I had left my purse on the screened porch back at the coast. I thought I would die.

"When I finally got up the nerve to tell my new father-in-law where my purse was, he clacked his teeth, took a swig of antacid, donned his hat, and headed back to the coast. It took only a few short years before he was able to see the humor in it."

Mother had done her job well. I *did* feel better about my own absent-mindedness. It was obviously in my genes! I also tried to imagine my dear granddad in the power position of a middle-aged man in his prime—and my parents as newlyweds. I wondered if it seemed a long time ago to them. Probably not.

With renewed patience I began pointing out things of interest to the children as we drove. Daddy joined in because he loved few things better than seeing sights and reading historical markers. As kids, David, Rachel, and I came to refer to them as "hysterical" markers, because upon seeing one, he often threw on the brakes with such force the three of us ended in a pile in the back of the station wagon. Just outside West Memphis, Arkansas, he spotted a large arena and slowed rather gently, I thought, for a site he seemed to find so fascinating.

"Hey, that must be where they race greyhounds," he remarked. Well, I had to admit, he had come up with something interesting this time.

"Buses?!" I said, sitting up straighter to rubberneck out the window. "They race *buses!?*"

He and Mother seemed to think that was awfully funny, and when he explained they raced greyhound dogs in the arena, I snapped, "I knew that!" but I don't think they believed me.

After one final supper stop at Kiddie Burger where Zach and Zeke let off steam on the playground while I nursed Baby Rachel in heavenly peace, we reluctantly piled back into the wagon and headed east with the sunset in our rearview mirror. Barring the unexpected (does the reader care to place bets here?), we would pillow our heads that night in Mother and Daddy's little bungalow in Virginia. At this point, I could have cared less about a nest of my own. I'd be delighted to snuggle with my brood of chicks in my parents' nest—as long as it wasn't on wheels.

With Trail Boss back in the saddle again, the herd fed and snoozing contentedly, he was ready to hit the asphalt trail once again. Nightfall brought with it blessed serenity as starlight illuminated the happy trails stretching out under the headlights of our fully loaded wagon.

Daddy brought a steaming styrofoam cup to his lips and paused for a quick second to inhale the rich scent of the coffee before partaking of a sip. After breathing out the "Ahhh" that always follows the first taste of good hot coffee, I'm pretty sure I overheard him whisper softly, "Yeeehaw! Let's bring this herd on home. And Lord, would you mind sending a couple of angels to ride shotgun the rest of the way?"

I have been constantly on the move. . . . I have labored and toiled and have often gone without sleep; I have known hunger and thirst and have often gone without food.

2 CORINTHIANS 11:26–27, NIV

Fowl Play:
A Feather in My Mother's Cap

As long as I live, I shall never forget (my brother and sister will never forget, my now-husband-then-friend-at-church will never forget, quite possibly the entire city of Arlington, Texas, will never forget) the days that my mother turned into a walking, talking, breathing, feathered chicken. Maybe I'm exaggerating, but only slightly so.

It was the early seventies, and other mothers had discovered what they called "petal caps," a nylon concoction designed to cover their hair before they knew what to call "bad hair days." My mother, however, purchased and wore, not the petal-covered variety, which in our eyes would have been more than enough. Oh no! She opted for one covered with white, farm-fresh chicken feathers. We told her it looked sick. She insisted she looked chic. We resorted to begging.

"Please, please, oh, heaven help us, *please* do not wear it in public," we begged. But she would have none of our squawking. Out the door she'd strut, feathered head held high with pilgrim's pride. There were moments back then when I felt certain my psyche would never, ever become unwarped, and there are those today who might say I had the diagnosis absolutely correct. Certainly, I vowed at the time, I would not make the same sort of traumatizing mistakes with my own children. Little did I know that by the time kids become teenagers, parents can embarrass them by simply breathing.

When children are small and Mommie is their world, it's a rather grand affair to own an eccentric, unsensible mother. In fact, for some few years, I saw myself as doing quite well as a mother. I recall a day when I went to pick up Zach and Zeke after a visit with a little friend. They were about ages six and five and climbed into the front seat of the car with twin looks of disgust and disappointment. Their evaluation of their social interaction period was somewhat less than satisfactory. Zachary was the first to voice the most serious complaint.

"Mom, it was raining outside. There were *great* mud puddles everywhere, and Jason's mother wouldn't *even* let us go outside to play in them."

I mirrored their disgust, donning an expression of surprised horror. At that point, little Zeke joined his brother in a synchronized nod. Then he looked up at me, his brown eyes radiating awe and appreciation.

"I'm so happy you aren't sensible like all the other kids' moms." I'm sure he thought he had handed me the compliment most likely to secure my place in the Mother's Hall of Fame, and I guess I *am* pretty proud of it. After all, it's in my genes. When I was a grade schooler, I felt I had a mother who was the envy of children far and wide. Well, at least down to the end of the suburban cul-de-sac where I lived. For starters, my mother was careful to teach us children an array of classical melodies, always sung in the voice of a wounded mezzo soprano. One of my favorite arias went something like this (sung to the tune of "Stars and Stripes Forever"):

Oh, be kind to your web-footed friends,
For a duck may be somebody's mother
Who lives all alone in the swamp

Where it's very cold and damp.
Oh, you may think that this is the end.
Well, it is.

As I write this, I'm moved to wonder what my mother's particular fascination with domestic fowl in this stage of her life might have indicated about her buried subconscious. At the time, however, I just enjoyed the fallout, and shared the song with my best friend, a very blue-eyed, very blonde girl named Allison who lived across the street. We sang it at the top of our lungs in ducklike, quacking voices as we walked arm in arm in a warm summer rain, splashing through puddles as we went.

If we were very, very good children we were sometimes treated to another royal performance by my mother. She would sit up very straight, adjusting her position so as to give us all the best possible view. Then, gesturing gracefully, she would rub her index finger against her front teeth until they were completely and thoroughly dry. This had to be done with painstaking care, or the stunt we were breathlessly awaiting would not work.

The grand finale came when she somehow managed to tuck her upper lip underneath itself, so that it stuck in that attractive position, revealing her gums and front teeth. She then completed her entertaining exhibition by rapidly raising and lowering her eyebrows, Charlie Chaplin style, while simultaneously flipping her tongue in and out of that crazed bunny mouth. In the end, she looked like some wild, animated rabbit. Could any child have wished for more?

As the teenage years approached, however, it was not always a many splendored thing to have a mother who was somewhat left of center, and I will just refer to the feathered hat this one last time and then try to put it behind me. Eventually our mother hen came to her senses, and the poultry wig ended up in the costume box. My siblings and I drew a collective sigh of relief, and in time even this suffering in our young lives emerged as pure gold. With the addition of longhandled underwear, a cone-shaped party hat for a beak, and a pair of yellow rubber gloves pulled over our toes for chicken feet, each of us kids won at least one first place award at a variety of costumed affairs.

That was the early seventies. In the nineties, I recall a fairly recent time when I forgot to wind up my wire-covered headband and tuck it into its decorative knot as required. When I drove to the mall and went inside to pick up my kids, the two ends of the headband were sticking straight up in the air.

As soon as the children spotted me, they grabbed me and hustled me into a dark hallway as quickly as possible, reminding me of the way I acted the day I discovered one of my toddlers playing outside in the buff. There they explained to me with indignation that their mother had showed up at the mall in our small town, where just *everybody* knows us, looking for all the world like a large beetle with two polka dot antennae sticking straight up in the air. I had the feeling they would have shaken me if they dared.

More recently, I have managed to humiliate my children simply by driving my car, which has 215,000 miles on its rusting body. As you can imagine, the appearance of the car itself would be embarrassing enough for them, but it also makes obnoxious and humiliating noises. How can I put this in delicate terms?

Let's try this: Often when I run into the Get-It-Kwik to buy a soft drink or candy bar (and use my credit card for the purchase; doesn't everybody?) the clerk usually asks me a question that takes me slightly aback.

"Do you have gas, too?"

"No," I respond, "that's just the way my car sounds. Sorry."

Last week, I drove my children through Taco Mucho and gave our order to the loudspeaker box. "What was that again?" the voice asked politely. Again I repeated our order. We continued our game of "Come again?" until finally, the exasperated voice said, "I'm sorry, Ma'am. We can't hear you over the noise of your car. Would you mind turning off the ignition?"

When I drove up to the window to pick up our mucho burritos, I discovered I seemed to be alone in the car. Looking down, I saw my four children piled on the floorboard like a stack of pancakes, trying desperately not to be seen by their peers.

I now know it is inevitable that I will mortify my kids no matter what I do. I've come to grips with that. They'll be fine. After all, just look what a functional adult *I* turned out to be. When they whine about cleaning up their messes, I pull out my "cheery working songs" repertoire. I have a lovely English version of Mary Poppins trilling, "A Spoonful of Sugar." I can also offer my personal favorite, sung with the voice of an over-achieving dwarf, "Whistle While You Work." If my teenage sons happen to have guests, they respond by cranking their radios up full volume and working like wildfire to escape the house. Yes. I know it's a cruel trick, but it's effective.

This spring, I visited my daughter Rachel's fourth grade class to encourage them to try writing, especially humorous stories. As a result, the class gifted me with a collective effort, a book titled *Lone Oak's Fourth Grade Funny Follies*, full of their funniest and most embarrassing moments.

It's priceless. But I was most anxious to read what my own daughter would write. After all, there are so many stories from which to choose when you happen to be a member of our family. I was to be honored with a mother/daughter story. It follows, exactly as Rachel wrote it:

One afternoon in November, my mother and I were driving to Wal-Mart in the van. I saw two ladies talking in sign language. I thought it was neet and told my mother. She said "let's try it." I replied "Mother I havn't been too bad latly have I?" She laughed as she did all these strange signs. I ducked under the dash. "Your'e imbarrising me mom and yourself." I said. But she said in a greedy voice "I don't get imbarrissed." I moaned and ducked lower as she went on with her sign language. As you might already know I get imbarrised easily (Especailly with my mom.)

by Rachel Freeman, age 10

Ah, the warm memories my daughter's story brought to mind. The times I offered to pay Mother not to sing in the car. The ridiculous way she exercised in her pink negligee each evening, rolling on the floor from hip to hip with her hands held out to the side like an elegant ballerina. The unsensible way she let us play in the rain and splash in the mud. The way she'd tackle unsuspecting babies, toddlers, fourth-graders and even teen-agers, smothering them with hugs and kisses.

This Mother's Day, I read an article in the May '94 issue of *Reader's Digest* that struck a chord with me. It was titled, "My Mother Barked Like a Seal." Great title, eh? Jeanmarie Coogan writes of her quintessentially embarrassing mom, finally pointing to a childhood memory of her mother passing by a tree where a "bunch of us were dizzily swaying in the top branches." Rather than shrieking with fear, Jeanmarie's mother said, "I didn't know you could climb so high." Then she added, "That's terrific! Don't fall!" As the mother walked away, one boy, writes Jeanmarie, "spoke for us all. 'Wow,' he said softly. 'Wow.'"

Like Ms. Coogan, I also noticed as a child how my "friends, silent in their own homes, laughed and joked with my mother." And I was also blessed with a home where teenagers congregated and their craziness simply added to the playful and ongoing banter.

Let's face it. Some of us were simply cursed with eccentric, erratic, embarrassing mothers. But, didn't we have *some* fun?

But God hath chosen the foolish things of the world
to confound the wise.

1 CORINTHIANS 1:27, KJV
෨

59

Any Game Birds
Up for a Sport?

Have you seen the pictures in magazines of Brother, Sister, Dad, and Mom-with-baby-attached, as they ride bicycles together and tour Vermont-looking country roads? The picture is always labeled, "The family that plays together stays together." I have always wondered what sort of caption would have gone under a picture of my family of origin just trying to mount and stay seated upon their respective bicycles. Probably, "Accidental Tourists Waiting to Happen."

During the gasoline crisis of the late seventies Mother became concerned that she was going to be stranded at home planting tomatoes in her useless gas-guzzler. She persuaded Daddy to invest in a bicycle for each of them, failing to mention that she had never *really* learned to ride one.

On their first outing on their new bikes, Daddy took off through the neighborhood, assuming his wife was peddling along behind him. He turned around just in time to see her nosedive off the bike onto the grass. When he went back to check on her, she assured him she was unhurt, and the fall had been a fluke.

"Not to worry," she said, remounting her bike and sticking her tongue out the side of her mouth in concentration.

"OK, here we go!" he said, and rolled away. Feeling like a kid again, he looked forward to a ride in the evening breeze. "How you doin'?" he called back to Mother over his shoulder. There was, once again, silence. Feeling a little more anxious this time, he wheeled around to see her sitting on the sidewalk, her teased bun definitely askew and her knee cap bright pink. She looked, shall we say, daunted.

"Why didn't you *tell* me you don't know how to ride a bicycle?!" he yelled.

"Well, it *looks* so easy," she said, as if someone had been deliberately deceiving her.

"Look, Evil Kneivel," Daddy said, "see if you can walk that thing back to the house without breaking your neck. There's more to riding a bike than meets the eye."

Consider our shock when somewhere about the time of the arrival of my fourth baby, my sister Rachel went hunting and bagged Scott St. John-Gilbert III. We then learned what a sports fan really is. Up until this time, Daddy had been only mildly interested in watching football games on TV, and I had frequently observed all the Arnold males gather enthusiastically around the television for a major game only to find them all snoring in chorus by halftime. Imagine our shock when gentlemanly Scott St. John-Gilbert—Gilley to me—joined our family and during our first TV football game together sent Mother almost through the ceiling with his bellows. They were not unlike that of a badly wounded water buffalo.

We have a sports fan on our hands who will arise at 6:00 A.M., run out on the porch in his skivvies in sleet and snow to bring in the sports page, check it out, and return to bed, quickly dropping back to sleep.

Gilley, a fanatical San Francisco 49ers fan, visited my parents one year in Texas when the 49ers were to play the Cowboys in Dallas, and, of course, he found that to be the opportunity of a lifetime. Gilley was not about to be intimidated by the fact he was totally surrounded by burly Cowboy fans. Mother told me later she was just thankful to get out alive.

As I have reviewed my family's sports history, I've been wracking my brain trying to think of one sport that I have ever played with my mother. I vaguely remember spending a day with Mother at Girl Scout camp where we both tried our hands at archery. After twanging our wrists several times with the string, almost poking each other's eyes out with the end of the bow, and watching our arrows arc a full twelve inches each time we shot, we gave it up and retired to the shade of a tree and to our favorite camping sport—whining about the heat, wondering when it would be time to roast marshmallows for our s'mores, and just generally wishing the Powers That Be would let us have my camping badge so we could go home to do our nails. But there was more to come.

At trail riding time, Mother's horse had her number long before she managed to mount him. You could almost see him yawn as he thought, *Oh, boy, I got another live one.* Once she was on board he promptly sat down and tried to roll over on her, and I must say, I was impressed with her leap to safety. That did it, however. We threw in the towel, went home to blessed air conditioning, gave ourselves a manicure, and became campfire dropouts. There are other ways in life to get to eat s'mores.

Some years later at a church camp, I "had the opportunity" to try horseback riding again. Needless to say, childhood memories caused me to be somewhat nervous that my steed might also stop, drop, and roll.

I found myself wishing there was something else more stationary than the horse to cling to and involuntarily grabbed an overhead branch as we were trotting along. Of course, the horse just kept right on going, and the branch, with me attached, slowly bent to the ground. I lay there in the dirt, flat on my back, and still holding the branch to my chest hollering, "Please don't step on me! Please don't step on me."

When no thrashing hooves ground me into the turf, I finally got up the nerve to open my eyes. There, silhouetted against the blue sky was my future brother-in-law, the Cowboy. He shook his head, said the cowboy equivalent of "Tsk, Tsk," and helped me up. And today, even though he has horses galore I could freely ride, I'm certainly thankful they don't depend on *me* for exercise.

By the time I had reached junior high, it was apparent I was never going to make any sporting-type team. To begin with, I always forgot at least part of my gym suit, and the punishment for this was that we didn't get to play anything which, as you can imagine, almost broke my heart. During one open house, my P.E. coach cornered my mother for a conference.

"Mrs. Arnold, Becky has forgotten her gym suit for three weeks in a row now, and if she didn't have such a cute little way about her, I'd wring her neck."

"Why, *thank* you!" Mother responded, feeling that in my case, a cute little way was going to be essential in getting me through life.

Even with my demonstrated lack of athletic ability, I usually got elected captain during basketball season because the captain of the team's duty was to make charts and decide whose day it was to play forward and whose day it was to play backward. Or something like that. Additionally, I've always been a diplomat of sorts, and I was able to make everyone as happy as possible with their position on the team whatever it happened to be. Then I stood on the sidelines and cheered "my girls" on with bits and pieces of sporting advice I'd heard from television commercials.

"Go, team, go! Push 'em back, push 'em back, waaaaaay back. We need a goal! We need a ball! We need a touchdown! Whatever you can get! Rah, rah, rah!"

At the end of eighth grade, my long-suffering P.E. coach gave out awards to the girls—most athletic, most sportsmanlike, etc. When I got my award, I wondered if it had ever been given before and might even have been created just for me. My award? Most feminine.

Daddy enjoyed sports and gave his best shot at teaching all three of us kids what he knew about basketball, baseball, track, etc. Needless to say, he had more luck teaching David and Rachel to catch and throw and run and make goals than he did his eldest. While David played respectable baseball, basketball, and golf, he'd much rather have thrown a lure in the mouth of a bass any day.

Rachel turned out to be a smackin' good softball player and played on the same team from fourth grade to high school graduation. Interestingly, Mother and Daddy both had a great time cheering for both Rachel and David during their baseball careers, and Mother either came to understand the game, or she did a great imitation.

"Way to watch! Way to watch!" she'd yell in a most un-feminine manner. "Good save! Bring her in home now!" I'd have never guessed she had it in her.

Come to think of it, our family did have *some* success at playing croquet, and occasionally even badminton, if we were not forced to break a sweat. Mother would also take us swimming and would actually get in the pool with us, but I never once, in all my life, saw her get a drop of water on her teased, bunned hair. It amazed me then, and it amazes me now.

Then, at age fourteen, something happened to change my life. Enter Scott Freeman, the nice muscular gymnast from church. When I went on my first ski trip with the church youth group, Scott and I were not yet an "item," and it would be months until we were, but big things were looming ahead. I was terrifically excited about the trip, and months beforehand I had obtained a permit to work at a fast-food seafood restaurant to earn enough money to go skiing in Colorado with my friends. Night after night, I had come home reeking of grease and fish, so when I hit the slopes, I was determined to get my money's worth. The first challenge was to figure out how to get my ski boots on and then to get them to stick to the skis. After an hour and a half of frustration, I started to cry. At that moment, who should come strolling by but the biggest sucker for a female tear in high school.

Scott saw me struggling, and though he had already been tearing up the slopes, he sat down to help me. At long last, he managed to get me up and out the door of the ski lodge with my boots secured to my skis. Unfortunately, I could not stay upright on them. An hour and a half later, we were still at the door of the ski lodge, and this time Scott was the one crying.

So it cannot be said that my husband didn't know what I was when he married me. Knowing full well what he had on his hands, he did it anyway, obviously not for my athletic ability. Maybe it was that "cute little way" thing.

When we had enrolled in college as newlyweds, Scott and I were determined to take as many classes as we could together—even the P.E. requirements. With Scott now having a more realistic understanding of my true athletic potential, we settled on a class in square dancing. Believe it or not, we loved it. For a couple of years, square dancing became a regular Friday night activity. We were one of about four young couples dancing with a room full of retirees. I guess that's where we both discovered we really enjoyed older people. They took us under their wings and out for pizza after the dance and generally treated us like one of the family.

We soon learned that square dancing is a whole world of its own, with competitions for the dancers and contests to judge the skill of the callers. The ladies wear gingham dresses with tiny little waists and enough eyelet embroidered petticoats to make the full skirts stand out at least two feet all the way around. The prescribed length is above the knee and it doesn't make any difference how old or young or plump or skinny that knee may be. The dresses were fun to wear, and we would have loved to jump right in with the square dance scene, but when I began having baby after baby it put a real damper on the whole experience. Have you ever seen a maternity petticoat dress? Not a "cute little" sight.

In our second year of marriage, Scott took me canoeing. That sounded sedate enough. Surely I could paddle down a lazy river without Olympic strength being a requirement. As we camped that night, however, it began to rain. In response, the sleepy Guadalupe river awoke with a start. The next morning, I reluctantly climbed in the canoe, and away we went—much faster than I expected. And much sooner than I expected, the boat turned over, and we were being dragged mercilessly through currents and rocks and ice cold water. Besides, my hair got wet.

When I finally bumped into land and climbed to safe refuge with the last ounce of my strength, I did what I always did on occasions that call for courage and strength of will. I laid down on the boulder and sobbed. In order to get me back to camp, Scott had to literally pick me up and force me back in the canoe. I am grateful to report that our bodies and our marriage survived the rapids, but I was far from a happy camper.

After ten years of raising little ones, Scott had long since earned his degree, and I decided to return to college for mine. I had one P.E. requirement left to fulfill and this time, I would not get to have the pleasure of Scott's company. I'm sure it must have broken his heart.

As it happened, the only class left open that fit into my schedule was a sport for which I had absolutely no interest—golf. My instructor turned out to be an aging ego-maniac who wore a gold chain and a silver toupee. It seemed to me that his goal for the semester was to spend as much time as possible talking about his golfing feats without ever having to actually teach us to play any golf.

After three weeks of listening to Coach Ego's monotonous soliloquy, we spent three more weeks in front of an instructional video tape. When we finally got to swing a club it was at Whiffle Balls in a gym. By the time I walked into the classroom for the final exam, I had never hit a real live golf ball at anytime during the entire course. I would have felt the venture had been money down the drain, but there was one small satisfaction. On the day of the final, I realized the instructor was nowhere to be seen—he'd been fired that week.

When Daddy heard I had taken a real college golf course, he was pleased and volunteered to take me out on the green to hone my skills. Daddy had played on his high school golf team, and was none too shabby, from what I've heard. On the day of our putting green date, he gave me patient and careful instructions.

"First, Becky, I'm going to teach you how to do some chipping."

I'd never heard of chipping before, but I felt I was a fairly quick learner. After all, there *was* that time I barely missed Daddy's head. Nearly "chipped off the ol' block," shall we say?

When we got to the putting green, I swung at the golf ball with the amount of force I had been accustomed to exerting with those Whiffle Balls in the gym. Daddy said it was the first time he'd ever had to yell "Fore!" on the putting green.

But even with the near miss during the chipping lesson and the "give 'er all you got" drive on the putting green, Daddy was a great sport and told me I did well for my first time out. Come to think of it, he never has offered to take me golfing again, but then, he's a busy man.

This past weekend, though, Daddy did call and ask if he could take Zach and Zeke golfing. He's bought the boys each a set of clubs and has spent some time with them at the driving range, sharing his expertise and his love of the sport with them. I'm sure it's because he saw the innate golfing talent in their mother and decided he'd better start training his grandsons early.

When the three of them got home, they were all laughing and smiling. They'd obviously had fun. Zach and Zeke were especially thrilled with being allowed to drive the golf cart. Daddy was still chuckling at their adventures.

"Ol' Zeke got behind the wheel of that golf cart and took off so fast my cold drink went up my nose and down my throat without me even having to swallow." Other fathers might have been irritated, but my dad thought it was hilarious. Obviously I had prepared him well for grandfatherhood.

Scott, Zach, and Zeke are currently trying to master sailboarding. Since all of our boats and motors are beyond affordable repair, it may be the only way they'll ever be able to get around the lake, short of swimming. The fellas can each manage to get the boat "out to sea" with skill and grace; it's the "back to shore" part that is the challenge. From the dock where the rest of us lounge and sip cold drinks, the boys look as if they are doing some slapstick comedy routine on a surfboard.

First, they get all situated, then they're off and gliding for about five seconds. That's when the huge sail bonks them on the head or pulls them forward, and overboard they go. This happens time and again for our nonstop viewing pleasure. Once, however, when Scott had set sail alone, he stayed so long in the middle of the lake I began to get angry.

"Scott!" I hollered, "quit fooling around and come back to shore! It's time for supper!"

He just kept waving at me from the middle of the lake and continued his sailing, ignoring my shouts. I was fit to be tied. After awhile he lay down on the board and relaxed, looking for all the world as if he planned to spend some lazy hours soaking up some rays and avoiding having dinner with his family!

I sat on the bank and steamed for an hour or so, and then I noticed he had hailed a fellow in a boat to come over in his direction. I must say I felt pretty bad when I saw the fellow tie a rope to the sailboard and start towing him to shore. The whole time he'd been waving at us, he'd been stuck and was actually waving for help. When he got to shore, he was completely exhausted. Well . . . he *looked* like he was having fun.

With my infamous lack of coordination, it's pretty amazing I've only had three sports-related injuries. First, I pulled a neck muscle teaching a group of fifth graders to do a Teenage Mutant Ninja Turtle rap dance. Then, I've suffered two sprained ankles.

I hate to admit it, but the first sprained ankle resulted when I had pulled up in our driveway and was trying to finish some convenience store ice cream before going in the house where all the kids would want a bite. As it happened, the dog wanted a bite and jumped up to lick my spoon, and I fell out the door of the parked car. The last injury occurred when I fell down a flight of stairs. Before you feel terribly sympathetic, I might mention there were only three steps in the "flight."

I guess there will always be a challenge for me when learning or teaching new athletic skills. It would have probably been easier for Scott if my mother had been able to teach me to dive like a graceful sea gull or sprint like an ostrich. But alas, Mother and I will forever belong to that category of fowl birds known as corny-ish game hens, or preferably, table-game hens. I know, baaaaaad joke. But it's *sort of* got a "cute little way about it," don't you think?

Wilt thou play with him as with a bird?

Job 41:5, KJV

69

When the Bough Shakes

During the time when Zach and Zeke were both in diapers and under the age of three, the unthinkable happened. My parents moved away to Virginia for three years. At the time of the move, they felt free to follow their dream. Their nest had emptied, their three living parents were elderly but in fair health, and I'm sure they thought Scott and I might take a breather from having babies for a while.

They had been in Virginia just eighteen months when my phone rang one evening. Mother's voice on the other end of the wire sounded tense.

"Becky, I've had news from your daddy's side of the family," she said. "Are you sitting down? Grandmother Arnold has been diagnosed with Alzheimer's disease!"

After the first wave of shock and sadness, my internal reaction to Mother's announcement was—*So, that's what's been wrong!*

When my mother took a mother-in-law at the tender age of nineteen, she had a less than realistic view of older women. For one thing, *her* mother (my Nonnie) was by then sixty-two years of age, and as I have indicated, Nonnie was then at her best and most mature self, approaching sainthood. Mother had assumed that all women everywhere mysteriously entered into sainthood somewhere around middle age. She had great difficulty understanding that her husband's mother, my Grandmother Arnold, was actually a cute little woman who had never grown up.

Mother spent the first twenty years of her marriage periodically fussing with my Grandmother Arnold, or Margaret, as Mother called her. Mother kept expecting her to be different from who she was, to give more than she could give—in short, to be like Nonnie. And I'll have to admit, even as a child I had to notice—my grandmother was a case, by almost any standard. Even when I was a little girl alone with her, I always had the oddest sense that I was the more grown-up of the two of us. Now, that wasn't always a bad thing to me. Actually, it was often kind of fun.

To me, Grandmother Arnold was jolly and huggable and too short to be intimidating, even to the smallest child. She was like a round, fluffy Chatty Cathy doll—only there was no "off" button behind her neck, and her batteries never ran out. But *I* was free to run out to play when I tired of her endless chatter. Mother, unfortunately, was not. On many of Grandmother's visits, I'm sure there were probably times when Mother would have gladly run out the door and joined me in climbing a tree.

The sound of Mother's voice on the phone brought me back to the crisis at hand. "I can't help wondering how many years this has been developing," she said. "How much of the self-centeredness and the temper tantrums were really beyond her control? We've all known for a long, long time that her behavior just didn't make sense much of the time." I heard a sigh, and we were quiet a moment, absorbing this new change now facing our family.

"What made them check for Alzheimer's?" I finally asked.

"Your Grandaddy Arnold—Lloyd—has been keeping so much of what was going on with them to himself. He's spent a lifetime protecting her and looking after her, and he loves her. He had become very good at seeing her unacceptable behavior as acceptable, and since his retirement, he devoted himself to getting her through the rest of life and trying to keep peace in the process.

"The last time they were here, I couldn't believe what their life together had become. Margaret could not sit still longer than a couple of minutes at a time, but she also couldn't get up and down by herself.

"'Honey!' she would say to Lloyd, 'I gotta get up. Help me up!' And frail as he was, he would haul himself out of his chair, take her hands, and pull her to her feet. She'd wander through the house five minutes or so, sit down for two, and then repeat the process.

"He was worn out, of course, but she didn't want anyone else to help. Many's the time I bit my lip to keep from saying, 'Just tell her no! Tell her to sit down and be still for a while!' Instead, he would fuss at her, but he always got up and helped her to her feet. Now, of course, I have read that wandering is a symptom of Alzheimer's. And that it goes on through the night.

"Even with this going on, though," Mother continued, "when they were visiting here not long ago, they still managed to keep some semblance of normal life going. I remember taking them shopping one day. Your grandmother picked out a ceramic mallard duck she wanted to buy for George, and she stepped up to the counter to pay for it. In the end, she had to give your grandad her purse so he could sort out the right amount of money to pay for it. It was so sad, but she was determined to do it, almost as if she were trying to prove to herself she was still OK. It reminded me of the bumper sticker that says, 'I shop, therefore I am.'"

I had to chuckle over that. "Do you suppose that will be the last major skill to go for most of us American women?"

"May be!" she laughed. "On that same shopping trip, a sweet thing happened for me, though. I admired a small cabinet in a craft shop, and Lloyd insisted on buying it for me. I never remember going shopping with my own dad or having him buy something just for me. It made me feel very special.

"After they went home, your Aunt Hazel and Uncle Buddy (Daddy's brother) called. They said Margaret and Lloyd reached a point where they were living on canned vegetable soup, and Lloyd was exhausted from lack of sleep. Still, he didn't tell anybody. But then his back began to go out on him, and eventually they both were on the floor and couldn't get up. Interestingly, it was your grandmother who managed to crawl to the phone and dial a friend."

"What will they do now?" I wondered. "They obviously can't go on living alone."

"Oh, they're already at Uncle Buddy's and Aunt Hazel's in Houston. Hazel said your grandmother came into the kitchen this morning and told her that the man in her bed was *not* her husband."

"Oh, my!" I laughed. "What did Aunt Hazel say?"

"She put her arm around Grandmother and told her, 'Well, let's look at it this way, Margaret. How many women your age have that kind of problem to worry about?'"

We chuckled, even in sadness, and then I asked how Daddy was taking the news. "He's brokenhearted, of course, but it explains so many things. *How* I wish I had been more patient with her through the years!"

"Mother," I interrupted, "you couldn't have known. No one could handle Grandmother for very long at a time without wanting to ask her if she wouldn't like to play the quiet game for a while."

"Thanks, honey," she sighed. "I may need to hear that again. I know there *were* some good times with her. I know when she agreed to let your daddy and I get married, I thought Margaret Arnold was so sweet I could have eaten her with a spoon. Six months later, I wished I had. She made most of the major mistakes it's possible for a mother-in-law to make. She talked about one daughter-in-law to the other and then reversed the process. When grandbabies began arriving, she let me know she did not want to babysit.

"'I'm the 'Going Grandmother,'" she said in her cutest baby talk voice. "*Your* mother is the baby-sitting kind." The odd thing is, she really liked Nonnie, as everyone did, and when she would be in trouble with me, she would call Nonnie for comfort!

"'Well,' Nonnie would say, 'I'm sorry you two have gotten crossways. Try not to let it worry you. It'll all work out.'" She had that incredible knack of not taking sides, yet being genuinely sympathetic to the emotional pain of both her daughter and her daughter's mother-in-law! No small trick!

"As Margaret grew older, she became so volatile and created such a tense atmosphere when she visited in our home that I had just about stopped inviting her to come. She became more and more unreasonable, self-centered, and demanding, and the talking never stopped. After a while, she even talked through the night in her sleep!

"It bothered all of her children and their spouses that it was next to impossible to have a conversation with Grandaddy because she never stopped talking. We could see him growing older and would have liked to know him better. We all imagined that he would have talked more of himself if she could have given him the opportunity.

"I'd like to believe that if I had known the Lord personally in the days when I was young I would have done better in my relationship with my mother-in-law," my mother sighed.

"When I think of the wasted hours I spent standing at the kitchen sink doing dishes and mentally stewing about our latest tiff. . . . I wish I would have had more compassion for my mother-in-law. This was a woman who desperately longed for intimacy, but for whatever reasons, she seemed locked inside the dome of self—the worst form of solitary confinement! She could see people, but she couldn't seem to mesh comfortably with them. And now I wonder if there has not always been some chemical or emotional problem that overwhelmed her. I suspect she has done the best she could in life," she finished.

I was quiet a minute, gathering my thoughts. Then I proceeded to put in my two cents worth. "Mother, I suspect you're right. I heard something recently: 'Hurting people hurt people.'

"Now let me tell you some of my memories of how you actually treated Grandmother. When they came to visit, I remember that you prepared Grandmother's and Grandaddy's favorite meals for them and how you greeted them as if they were honored guests. Maybe that's why they seemed to love to come and stay at our house. Have you forgotten that you knew her favorite fragrance, her favorite lingerie, and her favorite color for those birthdays, anniversaries, and special occasions she loved so dearly? I remember that you patiently entertained Grandmother with card games and endless conversations where you lovingly tried to explain to her how to have a relationship with Christ. And I remember your praying for her and for your relationship with her."

"It's amazing you would remember those things!" Mother marveled.

"Why do you say that?" I asked, suddenly feeling a bit defensive about my brain synapses. "I can remember *lots* of things."

"Say what?"

"What? I'm getting lost in this converstion!"

"Are you OK?" She sounded worried.

"I'm OK. You're OK. Where were we? Memory loss . . . Grandmother. Oh, yes. She did love a party, and you knew how to make even the smallest event a celebration—especially when we celebrated the April 16th birthday she and I shared. Hey, you even gave Grandmother her first grandaughter on her own birthday! But when she visited I also remember the gratitude I felt that I could go off to school for a quiet break. I looked back over my shoulder at you with sympathy. I knew you would be spending the entire day entertaining and placating the woman\child Grandmother was. I'd say you went above and beyond the call of duty."

I felt another pearl of wisdom, a timeless truth forming in my head. I plunged ahead, eager to share it.

"Isn't it true that almost everyone who has been through the aging and death of a parent lives with guilt? Erma Bombeck calls guilt, 'the gift that keeps on giving.' You didn't do things perfectly, but then you'd never been a daughter-in-law before, either."

"Becky," Mother answered, "thank you. I needed to hear that. I love you."

"I love you, too. Can I ask you a question before you hang up the phone?"

"Sure."

"Who *is* this?"

"Queen Elizabeth," came the voice over the wire—but at least she was laughing when she hung up.

Be kind and compassionate to one another, forgiving each other, just as in Christ God forgave you.

EPHESIANS 4:32, NIV

PART THREE

The Jones Roost

A Wise Owl with a Touch of Dove in Her

During a recent lunch date with Mother, the conversation turned to my Nonnie, her mother, the dear, greatly loved wise owl of the family tree who had shocked us all by growing old and ill. Somehow we hadn't expected it, and it made me feel more than a little blue.

"Tell me more of what she was like when you were growing up," I asked, sensing a need to capture and hold memories of her now in my head and heart.

"Well, to begin with, her two given names certainly hinted of fame and fortune. The first, as you know, is Elsie, and we kiddos always loved associating that name with a certain famous cow. There were *lots* of jokes about *that*. Her second name was Pearl. Elsie Pearl. Isn't that lovely? Her maiden name—Smith—was so commonplace she had the good sense to change it by marrying a man named Jones. Deacon, they called him.

"They had seven children in fourteen years, and the last three of us were born during the Great Depression. And of course you know that daddy was overwhelmed with the responsibility of it all. For that, and other reasons, he was often a bear to live with.

"I don't want to give the impression that life was always bleak at our house, because we had some wonderful times, usually when Daddy was away. I had five big brothers—George, Joe, J. R., Lloyd, and Genie—and every one of them was a comedian with a different style. Your Aunt Etta had arrived in the family second in line, and I brought up the rear.

"There were two things your Nonnie never intended to do—'bob' her hair or put on a pair of slacks. She always wore a print house dress and an apron, and the boys never passed her without untying the apron. She would laugh and scold and threaten to 'box somebody's ears,' but we always knew she loved the horseplay as much as the rest of us.

"When I was in junior high, my brother Joe fell from a rooftop where he was working and suffered a head injury. Over a period of months, his health deteriorated and to our heartache, he died in an iron lung in a charity hospital in Dallas. Nonnie went about doing what had to be done, and I only occasionally saw quiet tears spill from her lovely blue eyes. I never saw her break down, but whenever she spoke of him, her eyes always misted with tears. One thing I learned from her then was that all things in life can be borne. She brought Philippians 4:13 alive for me: 'I can do all things through Christ which strengtheneth me.' I consider those qualities of hers to be part of an inheritance from a mother who was rich in many ways other than money.

"We were always able to take Nonnie totally for granted in a wonderfully comforting way. We had very little of this world's goods, but we did have our mother. We knew she would be at home when we left for school and almost always at home when we came back at the end of the day. On the rare occasions when we came home and she wasn't there, the day seemed cold and uneasy until she returned.

"I remember as a young girl some of the expressions she often used that I now recognize were her 'gems of wisdom,' and they sometimes echo through my mind as if she were standing just behind me as I live my life even yet."

How interesting, I thought. *So my mother still hears her mother whispering over her shoulder, too!*

Mother continued, "Whenever I would suffer a great disappointment, Nonnie would say, 'Well, things have a way of working out for the best, Honey.' She was a great believer in 'getting busy,' and I remember her opinion about a nervous friend with tendencies toward hypochondria: 'I believe if she'd just get her mind off herself, she'd be all right,' Nonnie decided.

"Our mother gave us the absolute assurance that we were loved, that life at its darkest has moments of laughter and light, that nothing happens in life that cannot be borne with Christ's help. And her six remaining children have gone out into the world and achieved more successes than failures, and none of us has squandered his or her life.

"You remember the house we grew up in. When we moved into it, it was fifty years old, and I doubt it had seen the business end of a paint brush in all those years. It sat on the edge of a major highway and next door to a drive-in restaurant popular in the fifties. Grandaddy Jones would never have considered moving to another house, so when he died, the six of us adult children pooled our resources and bought Nonnie the house she always wanted there in our small town. It was white stucco trimmed in Dutch blue, and she quickly planted red geraniums around her picket fence. She has enjoyed it enormously.

"And so have we all. Some of you grandkids have gone there for her healing touch when you have been sick in body or spirit. Perhaps her greatest gift has been in knowing how to listen. Over the years we have always converged on her house for reunions and holidays, sometimes as many as thirty of us.

"None of us ever leaves without her standing by her picket fence, waving her work-worn hand as long as we can look back and see her. It's a pretty picture she makes in her flowered house dress and apron, her silver white hair gleaming in the sunshine." Mother smiled at me across the lunch table, "I can't imagine what it will be like without her when she is gone."

My mind recreated a vivid memory of when I was a teenager at one of those reunions at Nonnie's house. Mother and Daddy and all my aunts, uncles, and cousins were scattered around the living room on couches, lounging on the carpet or leaning against the walls. The setting sun cast rosy glows through silky sheer curtains and came to rest gently on Nonnie's face. She rocked contentedly in her comfy chair surrounded by her children and grandchildren. Softly, a male voice—one of my uncles—began to sing in deep baritone.

"When peace like a river attendeth my way." Raised in a church where the singing was a cappella, Nonnie and her grown children filled the room with rich harmony. "When sorrows like sea billows roll." The beautiful texture of the well-loved hymn saturated the room with a holy Presence. "Whatever my lot, Thou hast taught me to say, it is well, it is well, with my soul." Times of serenity, times of suffering. It is well, it is well. Because one day, "our faith shall be sight." On that day, the hymnist's words, full of come-what-may confidence, declare, "The trump shall resound, and the Lord shall descend. Even so, it is well with my soul."

I knew then, that no matter what the future might hold, the roots in our family tree would hold. Nonnie had tilled the soil well for faith to grow. And in the final analysis, things *do* have a way of workin' out for the best.

She speaks with wisdom,
and faithful instruction is on her tongue.

PROVERBS 31:26, NIV

A Bird in the Hand
Is Worth Two in a Rage

On the way home from that reunion, it occurred to me to ask about my Grandaddy Jones, who had died when I was in grade school. I remembered him as an elderly fellow dressed in khakis. He had a fascinating workshop in his garage and seemed to love for us children to explore it. The relationship between him and my folks had seemed warm, but I sensed from remarks among the Jones family that their early life with him had not been easy. Mother had promised to tell me; we had a long drive ahead of us, and it seemed like a good time to ask.

"From listening to your family, you'd think you all never did anything but create material for tall tales to tell at future reunions. Was it really as much fun as it sounds growing up with that bunch?"

"We had *lots* of fun, lots of the time," she smiled, "and if your Grandaddy Jones had not had a serious problem, it would have been fun *most* of the time.

I knew he had been eccentric. I had already heard some wonderful stories at the reunions about him. This was the grandaddy who in his twilight years flatly refused to pay a barber to cut his hair and did it himself. He merely grabbed a top knot of faded auburn hair, held it straight up, and then shaved all the hair around the edge. Once he brushed the remaining top knot down over the shaved area, it actually didn't look bad. Mother filled in more details of Grandaddy Jones' interesting habits.

"When he developed a toothache, he refused to pay the dentist," she laughed. "He tied a string around the offending tooth, tied the other end of the string around the bumper of their 1930 model car—this was in 1970—and tried to persuade Nonnie to drive the car down the alley behind their house.

"I thank God for the good memories I *do* have of him," Mother continued. "The best are from my preschool years. He was a nice-looking fellow as I remember and seemed ten feet tall when he swung me up to his shoulders for a ride. I used to wait for him to come home from work in the evening. I'd sit by the side of the dirt road leading to our house out in the country, piling mounds of sandy red soil on top of my bare feet until I spied him coming over the hill dressed in his khakis. I'd run to meet him and get to view the world on the way to the house from atop his broad shoulders. Each evening he walked home from a ten-hour day as a carpenter, his fair skin burned red from working under the blazing sun all day. The Great Depression was just ending, and his pay was pitifully low. I was his seventh child, so he carried the heavy load of supporting a large family.

"Most evenings he stretched out on his bed with the daily paper and let me comb, braid, and pin curl his wavy auburn hair. And if the evening was really warm, he might stretch out on the bare wood floor in front of an open door to catch the evening breeze. My brother Genie would lie on one of his outstretched arms and I on the other while he told us *wonderful* stories. A favorite of mine was about his imaginary other family who lived off in the wilds, and I never doubted for a minute it was true. The mother was a wild woman who roamed through the prairie with a passel o' kids, all barely clothed, howling like a banshee in the wind. Here he would do a wonderful imitation that fairly set my hair on end. This was so real to me that I began to save pennies for him to buy clothes for them on his next trip to visit them. When Genie told me he was just making it up, I felt as if I'd lost part of my family!

"But then an evening came when he appeared to me to be sick at the supper table. I must have been about five years old and always sat on a bench at the table between Genie and Lloyd, the two youngest of the five brothers. Daddy seemed terribly sleepy that night and stumbled when he walked. And his table manners were terrible. I remember it being awfully quiet during the meal, with Nonnie moving around the table to serve us. Her face was sad, and she said almost nothing. Only later did I learn that this tiredness and clumsiness came from a bottle.

"After that, there were many times when we went through long periods of his drinking, and with that drinking came violent outbursts of temper when the older kids had it pretty rough. Sometimes Nonnie took the brunt of it. Over the years, I suppose each one of the seven of us had at least one encounter with him when we actually did hand-to-hand combat."

Oh, Mother, I didn't know . . .

"Because of his drinking bouts, he was often unable to work, or there was no carpentry work in our small town. So, of course, there was never enough money, and we were always among the poor people of the town. When each of us kids grew old enough to work, we took our turns helping to put red beans, milk gravy, and fried potatoes on the table. Gradually, a blazing rage and hatred against him settled in me, and even after he stopped drinking when I was in high school, I would hardly stay in the same room with him.

"Nonnie always made sure we kids went to church with her every Sunday, and even though it was pretty legalistic, as you know, we certainly grew up knowing right from wrong. I had that strong moral sense that served me well as a teenager, but no personal acquaintance with God Himself, so there was no little self-righteousness in my attitude toward my father."

At this point, I had to ask how she and her family managed to function in that tense environment. Mother thought for a second and explained.

"Well, Daddy was a recluse and spent hours in his old workshop in the garage. We managed to have a great time when he would leave the house. He stopped taking his meals with the family somewhere along the way and stayed in his bedroom, so we were free to laugh, talk, and cut up together at meals.

"Your Uncle George, the oldest, bought the old house we were living in with a G.I. loan, and he was a strong presence among us. He would often announce supper by yelling, "Soup's on! All feet on the floor and no stabbing above the wrist!" This precipitated a near stampede, because at one time, nine of us gathered regularly around our supper table. Later on, it complicated matters when I began to court a fellow who was also named George, but my life turned a whole lot sweeter, any way you look at it.

"Nonnie was as hospitable as my father was inhospitable, and in spite of the poverty, she could somehow come up with meals for our friends who didn't mind visiting the unpainted old house on the edge of the highway, even with cars and trucks whizzing by day and night. And George Arnold, who lived in a little white house not nearly as close to the railroad tracks, didn't even seem to notice.

"Nonnie was always a great comfort to me, throughout some very tough years. She brought light into the gloomy house just by being in it. We all loved and respected her for her gentle ways and would have never hurt her on purpose, so there were not too many wild oats sown, even by her five sons. She got us through it all somehow."

I thought about the successive graduation pictures of three of my uncles, mother's brothers They were all wearing the same suit. I suddenly realized that life had not been easy for this family. But how did they keep smiling? I'd heard so many tales of laughter and fun.

"Of course," she went on, "the boys loved to have belching contests, which set my sister Etta's nerves on edge worse than just about anything they could have done. Usually at least one of them would finish a meal, stand, and belch 'til the roof rattled, give a horse laugh, and run down the hallway with her in hot pursuit. Uncle Genie tried it one day, though, and she changed her tactics. As he turned to run, she took her dinner fork and flipped it at him, not really meaning to hit him. That fork stood straight up in the calf of his leg! She was as shocked as he was and helped bandage him. As the second oldest child, she helped get Lloyd, Genie, and me through high school before moving away on her own.

"Since I was the youngest, I spent my senior year in high school at home in a house that had grown quiet after the older ones had made their way into the world. It was quiet, that is, until your Grandaddy Jones and I would lock horns. He had quit drinking by then, and it had been a long time since any of us had needed to be afraid of him. He had sobered up, but it was a little late in life to make a new start, so there was never really enough money to take a deep breath. I worked from junior high age on, just as we all had done. I resented him, and all the lost years, so he and I frequently said blistering things to each other and stormed in and out of rooms, slamming doors until the entire house shook, and Nonnie put her fingers in her ears. This was the state of our relationship when I left home to marry your dad.

"We moved to Lubbock so your dad could go to Texas Tech, and I missed Nonnie terribly that first year. We went home almost every weekend to visit in the old ramshackle house where they were still living. When I would come into the room where my father was, I expected him to leave it. And he did. I was still so furious with him that I failed to notice he was no longer fighting me. He simply did what I expected him to do, which was to stay out of my way. And then one day, in the space of five minutes, everything changed.

"We had been home for the weekend and were loading up on Sunday afternoon to go back to Lubbock. I went to the car to load my overnight bag and stepped back up onto the front porch, planning to go back into the house and hug Nonnie goodbye.

As I looked into the hallway, I saw my dad walk by Nonnie and say something to her I couldn't hear. He put his hand into her apron pocket and then passed on to his bedroom. She came out onto the porch with a strange look on her face, reached into her pocket, and handed me a five dollar bill.

"'Daddy asked me to give this to you and to tell you it's part of what he owes you,' she said carefully, as if she didn't quite know what my reaction would be.

"At first I was shocked. He was such a proud man, and there had been *so* much anger between us. I had never known him to humble himself before anyone. I don't remember what I said to Nonnie, but I got into the car with George, and we drove back to Lubbock. By the time I got there, all traces of anger and bitterness toward my dad had disappeared. I immediately sat down and wrote him a long letter telling him so.

"At the time, I didn't realize what a miracle had taken place in him and in me. I think of my relationship with God back then as 'long distance,' and it would be several years yet before I knew the reality of His love and presence in my life. Of course, once we have a personal relationship with God, we're able to look back and see very clearly how He was working, but at the time, I took the very wonderful change in my emotions as a normal thing. Daddy was sorry for what he had done, and I was glad—*very* glad—we were friends again.

"And the next time we made a trip home, he was watching the front door for us. He gave me a big hug and spent the weekend talking our ears off.

"From that point on, he always seemed childishly happy to see us, and when you kiddos began arriving, he was glad to send Nonnie to stay with us after each of you were born until I was on my feet again, though I know he missed her." My mother's face now reflected a sense of peace, certainty, and warmth.

"That's quite a story," I pondered aloud.

Mother smiled. "I've often wondered what my life might have been like if I had tried to live it with hatred in my heart against my dad. Even with our reconciliation, I had more than enough to deal with as an adult living with the consequences of so many years with an alcoholic father. I'm so glad he found a way to say, 'I'm sorry, Ruthie.'

"Years later—after your grandaddy died—after I invited Christ into my life, He gradually and gently led me to see that I had some things to apologize for, too. My rage and bitterness as a teenager toward Daddy were certainly natural, but I'm not proud of them. Christ cares about everything that happens to us, but He also cares about how we react to them. His desire is to enable us to react as He would—supernaturally. Of course, as a human being and especially as an adult who has been hurt as a child, we find it hard to look at our own shortcomings in such situations. Did I not have a right, after all, to my anger?"

I couldn't comprehend the difference between the kind of father I had been able to enjoy and the kind of father my mother had had. Yes, I think I'd have been *very* angry in her circumstances and probably would have felt that I had a right to it.

"It may not make much sense," she said, "but a lot of Christ's commandments are complete opposites of our natural inclinations. 'Love your enemies.' 'Do good to those who hate you,' and so on. The odd thing is that His way works so well. I owned up to my failures—the hurtful ways I reacted to my father's faults and asked forgiveness. Of course, your grandaddy was already gone by then, so I asked God for that forgiveness. And knowing that I *am* forgiven has given me a sense of peace when I look at the past." Mother paused for a minute and then continued.

"I'm just very thankful to God that I was reconciled to my dad before he died." She smiled, and her eyes grew moist. "It's made a great difference."

I couldn't help wondering how much of Mother's very obvious joy in life depended on that simple gesture my grandfather had made when he slipped a five dollar bill into Nonnie's pocket to pass on to his angry daughter. It wasn't much money, but he didn't have much then. But oh, the wealth he was able to give his daughter—and her future family—that day.

Honor thy father and thy mother; which is the first commandment with promise; That it may be well with thee, and thou mayest live long on the earth.

EPHESIANS 6:2-3, KJV

THIRTEEN

When Goosey Loosey and Henny Penny Meet for Lunch

The phone rang, interrupting my thought just before I could capture it on my computer screen. *Oh, pooh,* I thought, *I might not get another one today!* As soon as I heard the voice on the other end of the line, however, all irritation vanished. The caller was Shawn, one of my dearest friends. Soon we were both giggling, but I heard a sigh of exhaustion at the same time.

"Becky, I need to laugh. Can we have lunch together this week?" she asked. For myself and for most women I know, lunching and laughing has been *the* cure-all for the occasional blue funk, replacing the therapuetic "buying a new hat" our grandmothers used. So I jumped on the invitation like a duck on a june bug.

"Yes! I need a break, big time. Listen, I went to this little tea room in Arlington called the—oh, shoot—what was it called? It was English sounding. Winsome, Winded, Winsor—yes, I think it's called the Windsor Something. Why don't I call and make reservations and see if Brenda can join us, too?"

Thirty-odd years ago, my mother had started a healthy tradition by showing me what a powerful and enjoyable source of strength and healing friends can be in our lives. Not only did she show me, but she shared her friendships with me.

After talking to Shawn, I hung up the phone, still struggling to remember the name of the restaurant and finally dialed information and asked for a Windsor House. The operator gave me the number, and soon I was speaking to a genteel older woman.

"Excuse me, ma'm," I said politely. "I need to make reservations for three at your tea room." Her answer sounded like a script out of a sitcom, but I swear I am reporting exactly what this woman said.

"Honey, you've got the wrong number. You've reached a home for people who suffer from long- and short-term memory loss. I think the name of the place you're looking for is called, 'Out to Lunch.'" Perfect.

Does every woman have friends they just *can't wait* to see so they can tell them the "latest"? My first attempts to write humor would probably never have materialized if I hadn't enjoyed the comraderie of my girlfriends. They almost made me long for wild things to happen so I could come to the luncheon table on equal footing, bringing with me the quality of stories we had all come to expect from each other—stories to make us lay our heads on the table and beat it helplessly with our hands, lost in silent mirth; stories forcing us to hold on to each other's arms to keep from falling out of our chairs right there in the restaurant.

Early in our friendship Brenda summed up the feelings of us all when she blurted, "I *love* to laugh." It reminded me of the scene from *Mary Poppins*, where Mary's gentleman friend and the children float to the top of the room because they are laughing so uncontrollably. Wouldn't it be a kick if that were possible? When I get to heaven, one of the things I'm counting on is getting to laugh upside down on the ceiling of my mansion.

My mother was once again the role model/mentor for me in teaching me how to squeeze the most out of Lunch with the Girls. Some of my earliest memories are of playing in the yard of the student housing where we lived while my mother and her girlfriends kept a lazy eye on us and giggled in the sunshine. In cold weather, they often played cards while half a dozen or so of us kids played underneath the table and around their feet.

On hot summer days, the sound of the popsicle man driving by in his "Pop Goes the Weasel" truck created near panic among us. What if he went by before we could get permission and a nickel? Thankfully, our moms usually came through for us, and after the truck pulled away, I would sit on the front porch with my neighborhood buddies, licking the sticky grape coldness.

I had a feeling of belonging and security just knowing I was a part of this happy community of women and their children. When we heard our mothers laugh out loud through the screen door from the kitchen, we knew that all was right in our sunlit world.

Time passed and I grew up and married, but for an awkward while I was stuck in a no-man's-land as far as female companionship was concerned. I was just seventeen, too young to really feel a part of the upwardly mobile women in the young married class at church. At the same time, since I was a married woman, I felt out of sync with the teenage girls my own age. So in the in-between years, Mother and her friends often adopted me into their lunch group. I ate it all up—the food, the conversations, the gossip, and most of all, the laughter.

One of my favorite of my mother's friends is Almedia—dear, precious Almedia. She knows the best books to read, finds the perfect cards to give, searches out the hottest bargains in town, and owns a deep but lilting Louisiana laugh. I've watched her and Mother through the years, laughing their way through seasons of serenity and seasons of crisis, and I've learned the critical therapuetic value of a good lunch buddy.

When our first book came out, I came home one afternoon to find the following message on my recorder from Almedia, which I copied down because it was my very first "fan" message, and I was afraid I might not get another one.

"Becky," the voice said, "I just finished reading yours and your mother's darling book, and I'm just so full. Full of laughter and tears all at the same time. I always knew you were special and would do special things." When she heard Mother and me on a radio interview in Arlington, she drove up to the studio—while the live show was in progress—and tapped on the window. After we were off the air, she handed me a set of earrings she had just found at a boutique around the corner. "They were calling to me," she laughed. "They were saying, 'Buy us for Becky!'" And then, like the good fairy, she was gone.

We've all heard the saying, "The best way for a father to love his children is to love their mother." Well, I'm thinking about making a new cross-stitched saying, "The best way to love a friend is to love her children." Mother's close friends seem to have very naturally loved me and my brother and sister and continue to inquire regularly as to how we are doing. I feel that my best friends' children are partially mine and vice versa. The more adopted "aunties" in the world, the healthier our nation's kids. Hey, there's another saying to cross-stitch!

As I've come into adulthood, it's been fun to occasionally introduce Mother to friends of mine and watch her become quickly absorbed into our group. One such group originated when I felt the need to talk with a real author about the business end of writing and publishing. I learned of a lady in Greenville, a local author named Fran Sandin, who had written a touching book about coping with the death of her eighteen-month-old son. It was sensitively titled *See You Later, Jeffrey.* I bought her book and cried my way through parts of it—and yet it was so filled with Scripture and the loving comfort of God, that I couldn't wait to meet the Fran behind the precious words.

I had a hunch after reading Fran's book, and my hunch proved correct. I've found Fran both beautiful and sweet, one of the kindest and most thoughtful people I believe I've ever met. To myself, I teasingly and lovingly refer to her as St. Francis, although she would hate being looked upon as such. Even though she's survived a mother's nightmare, she talks about wanting to write a book called *Delighted with God.* Does that not speak volumes about her outlook on life?

Fran introduced me to Gracie Malone, a warmhearted easy-to-be-with woman who counsels and teaches younger women. Gracie had a desire to write, plus the skill and determination to get the ball rolling. The three of us found we were all in need of encouragement and motivation to get our manuscripts polished and in the mail, so we began monthly lunch meetings to pray and "talk writing" to our heart's content. All this "business" takes place over sandwiches, chocolate, and gourmet coffee at Mary of Puddin' Hill's, a charming Greenville tea room.

The first time I got together with Fran and Gracie, I asked Gracie for a ride home. A short time later, my phone rang.

"Becky, this is Gracie Malone. You didn't by any chance pick up my portfolio and notebook when you got out of my car, did you?" Of course, I had, and she has since told me she knew then ours was going to be a "fun" relationship. We've been laughing together ever since.

I recently emceed a ladies retreat where—get this—it was *my* job to keep everyone organized. Gracie, a veteran retreat speaker, came to my aid by attending the retreat. She followed quietly behind me, checked for my purse, encouraged me, and basically helped me stay on track through the weekend. My contribution to our friendship—besides keeping us laughing—is to encourage Gracie's writing talent and help brainstorm ideas for titles and projects. When Gracie called me this spring to say her first article had sold to *Moody Magazine,* I shed tears of joy as I hung up the phone. It's a writer thing. Or maybe it's a woman thing. Oh, I don't want to discriminate, maybe it's just a friend thing.

When I asked Mother to join Fran, Gracie, and me for our monthly lunch at Mary of Puddin' Hill, it was clear we would soon be a foursome. Not far into the lunch, Mother and Gracie discovered that Gracie's husband, Joe, had grown up in Mother's hometown of Sweetwater, Texas. They got so excited I thought we just might be the first ladies ever expelled from Mary of Puddin' Hill for disorderly conduct. Having found they shared West Texas roots, the two of them jabbered on and on like old pals. A few days later Gracie and I talked about the meeting.

"I just love your mother," she said enthusiastically.

"Yeah, she's pretty great," I answered teasingly. "But—so what am I now? Chopped liver?"

Gracie hugged me and laughed. "Honey, I love you, too."

"OK, then," I pouted just a tad. "I'll share." In all honesty, it's been a joy to see other women friends enjoy Mother as much as I do. I guess it's a sort of pay back for those days as a young bride when her friends became my friends, too.

But back to my greatly anticipated lunch date with Brenda and Shawn. It proved to be well worth waiting for. I pulled my station wagon up in the parking lot; Brenda soon followed. It dawned on me that we've been friends for seventeen years. But then, like minds have a way of clicking together right away and then hanging on for dear life through the years.

Once inside the beautiful restuarant, Brenda and I settled into our chairs, placed the melon-colored napkins in our laps, and sipped our water with slices of lime floating in the crystal goblet. The restaurant had not opened for lunch until 11:15. It was a late start. If it had opened earlier, I might have set our lunch date to begin at 8:30 A.M. just to make sure we had plenty of talking time. I was the first out of the starting blocks.

"So, Brenda, tell me about your new house and your new nursing job."

"Well," Brenda drawled in her wonderful southern accent. "I made 98 on my nursing exam yesterday. They said it was the highest score they'd ever seen. And then a few minutes later I couldn't figure out how to get a piece of plastic medical equipment apart, and the head nurse had to tell me it was all one piece. Becky, how can I be so smart and act like such a dingbat?"

Ah, a girl after my own heart. There aren't many of us—the tried, the true. With Brenda, I can relax.

Shawn joined us, only one hour late. We always allow each other one hour plus or minus scheduled appointment times, so Brenda and I never worried that she might not show up. As with Brenda, I did a quick tally of the twenty plus years Scott and I have known Shawn. She and Scott had actually grown up on the same block as kids.

Shawn's always been good for carrying more than her fair share of lunchtime laughs and table-slapping stories. Even during the black months when her husband left her because "she had gained weight, and he couldn't find a clean sock," she continued to be the epitome of those individuals who know how to make lemonade out of lemons, to bloom where you are planted, to make the most out of the circumstances, and just about every other "thought for the day."

It didn't take long for a good-hearted, handsome Christian man who loved children to scoop up Shawn with her bubbly personality and ask her to marry him. I remember well a phone conversation with Shawn on a summer afternoon in June.

"Becky, do you know a preacher near you who could marry us tomorrow maybe down by your lake?"

"What about your big wedding plans?" I asked.

"We'll still go through with the church wedding as planned in a couple of months. But we are ready to be husband and wife *now!*"

"Well," I was thinking hard, "the man who washes dishes for me when I cater dinners said he used to be a preacher. Would he do?"

"Perfect," she said. "And you can sing something pretty, can't you?"

"Um. Shawn. You *are* kidding about this, aren't you?"

"Nope. See you tomorrow night."

To make a long story short, I convinced my ex-preacher/dishwasher friend to perform an outdoor wedding ceremony "to go." Mary and Gary, other friends of ours, happened to drop by for coffee, and as soon as hasty introductions were made, they provided "the audience." The vows were short, but very sweet. As the breezes coming off the lake blew gently around the lovestruck couple, I sang, "God, a Woman, and a Man." When the preacher pronouced them man and wife, it dawned on me that I had just pulled together a wedding in twenty-four hours. What we won't do for our friends.

After the ceremony, we all walked up the hill to our house. I had thrown together an angel food cake from a mix, slathered it with Cool Whip and called it a wedding cake. I handed the new couple a knife to cut the cake and posed them so Scott could take a snapshot. When they applied knife to cake, it reminded me of a kid stepping on an inner tube. The cake collapsed every time they tried to make an incision—but over and over again it kept springing back up. With each attempt Shawn lost more control over her giggles. The newlyweds couldn't, for the life of them, get the knife to penetrate their wedding cake. They finally gave up and tore off pieces with their bare hands.

Now, five years later, we were eating lunch together and still laughing about the "tube" cake. By the time we left the restaurant, it was 2:20 P.M. I couldn't believe three hours had flown by so quickly. I felt deeply refreshed and ready to face real life again.

I'm convinced we would save enormous amounts of money on therapy in this country if more people would simply go "out to lunch" on a regular basis—preferably with friends who are also a little "out to lunch." And some tube cake now and then won't hurt either.

There is a friend who sticks closer than a brother.

PROVERBS 18:24, NIV
෮

The Freeman Perch

Feathering Our Messy Nests
with Memories

I love it that my mother-in-law, Beverly, is messy and disor-
ganized. I love it that she has never claimed to be a great cook.
It has relieved me of a tremendous amount of pressure in at least
one area. Since a can is a can is a can, Scott has never been able
to say, "Gee, honey, your green pea soup doesn't taste exactly
like my mom's green pea soup."

I have also had the great good fortune to marry a man whose
mother has, for the most part, been a less than enthusiastic
housekeeper. Now, when push comes to shove or there's a party
coming, Beverly can dust and straighten up and entertain with
the best of them. But let's face it, neither she nor I were born
compulsive cleaners. For better or for worse, my children (her
grandchildren) also appear to have been born minus the compulsive cleaning disorder gene.

In fact, my oldest son, Zachary, and I were discussing the
family tendency to be messy last night. He told me that at camp
this summer his cabin was so sloppy his roommates had to dig
through piles to find doors. He described their plan to placate
the counselor/room inspector.

"We put a sign up a sign that said, 'We are too busy practicing godliness to have time for cleanliness.' Then we left him a cold canned drink."

"Did it work?" I asked, impressed.

"Nah. The counselor pointed to the sign and to the room and yelled 'Blasphemy and bribery!' at the top of his lungs. But he did drink the Coke."

As with Zachary, Bev and I would love to be able to snap our fingers and have everything fall into place in our living quarters. Bev struggled with the guilt of being a "relaxed" homemaker for a long time, and then came to her moment of truth a few years ago. She made the announcement to her family with a mixture of pride and relief.

"I have given housekeeping a good, twenty-five year try." Having had an interest in art over the years, she decided to direct her energies into learning and exploring more creative avenues. Since then I've never had to worry about sprinting around my house spiffing it up before a visit from Bev. For this fact alone, I'm the envy of daughters-in-law the world over.

True to her newly announced goals, Bev became one of those brave women who return to college in mid-life and discovered she excelled, especially in the area of photography. Her new-found skill not only brought her creative talents out in the open but proved to complement her husband Jim's passion for cross-country motorcycling perfectly.

As she and Jim explored the nooks and crannies of small town America, her eyes were ever open for that perfect wildflower or rustic barn to shoot—with a camera, not a shot gun. (Sometimes these things have to be spelled out in Texas.) Because of her skill, we were also privileged to have a "pro" on hand to photograph all major family events. Just before I had my first child, Beverly inspired me to take a class in photography as one of my college electives. It proved to be one of the most useful courses I've ever taken. As a result, we do not bore our friends with mere "snapshots" of the grandkids. Bev and I think the brag books we have created are high quality portraits, thank you very much.

Currently, my mother-in-law is stretching her wings in the area of watercolor painting. Whatever she still lacks in house-cleaning, *I* think she makes up for in the beauty she brings to canvas—though she would beg to differ. She told me of a recent art lesson when the experienced "professional" teacher bent over her painting and loudly gave his critique.

"All I can say is less, less, less and bigger, bigger, *bigger!*"

"I wanted to yell back, 'What exactly does that mean, mean, *mean?*'" she sighed.

Once again inspired by Bev, I, too, decided to dabble in paint. Pouring over stacks of her "Decorating Ideas" magazines, I came across the old, "paint with crumpled newspaper" idea. Let me just say the boys' bedroom walls looked marvelous. So did their wood work, mirror, and finally, their carpet. When my preteen sons stared at their speckled room in disbelief, I felt I had to come up with an explanation—one they would believe. Actually, the answer came to me as a gift.

"It was Grandma's idea," I heard myself say.

How many daughters-in-law have a mother-in-law who insists on leaving the dirty dishes in the sink so she can jump in the lake for a swim or organize a game of croquet with the kids? She's coming out this weekend to teach Gabe to swim, as she has taught most of her other grandchildren. Recently, a good friend of Bev's told me, "I've never met anyone with as much natural talent as Bev, especially when it comes to teaching others a skill." Perhaps her choice to follow the road to development and growth hasn't always come easy, but she has unending patience with those whom she occasionally teaches.

On several occasions, Beverly has treated a grandchild to a afternoon of learning to draw on the "right side of the brain." I'd always taught my children not to draw on the walls or the wrong side of a piece of paper, but it never entered my mind they should be taught to draw on the right sides of their brains. Leave it to grandmas . . . .

Though Jim's and Bev's kids are grown, they both continue to provide opportunities for us to get together as a family—to make memories. This spring Jim and Bev invited Scott and his brother Kent to come up to join them for a weekend of skiing—encouraging the "boys" to get away, have some fun, and just hang out together. And there have been motorcycle trips, outings to the Glenrose Blue Grass Festival, tickets to the Harlem Globetrotters, the theater, and the circus. On an outing to Six Flags Over Texas, Jim wore a sweatshirt that read, "I'm celebrating my sixtieth birthday with my eight grandchildren at Six Flags Over Texas."

Through all these experiences, Jim and Bev provided fun ways for their adult children, their spouses, and their grandchildren to enjoy each other's company and, in the process, create warm memories. But there is nothing quite to compare with the celebration of Christmas at the Freemans.

To Beverly, Christmas isn't Christmas without a minimum of three Christmas trees, a warm hearth, poinsettias, old-fashioned holiday cards, ivy—a veritable "Chestnut's Roasting on an Open Fire" picture. It's important to her to make the season special, especially for her grandchildren. To accomplish that, she always arranges something unique—a genuine "memory maker"—each season.

One year she wrote a letter to each of the grandchildren about a memory she had of Christmases from her childhood and read them each aloud around the tree. This year we began our Christmas Eve morning at the ice-skating rink at the beautiful Tandy Center in downtown Ft. Worth. Her daughter and daughters-in-law may have been too faint of heart to attempt the ice ("We're getting too old!"), but Grandma Bev was out there skating as if this is what all grandmothers do.

When we returned to her exquisitely decorated home, there was even more fun in store. She and I had worked on a script together a few days before Christmas which would involve each of the grandchildren. Bev came up with the theme—acknowledging our ancestral roots in the celebration of Christmas. She had suggested the format, too—a talk show. The kids acted out a variety of characters including Rush Humbug; Zachenauger and Zekenauger, the twin weight lifters from Sweden; Real Texan Ross Perot; Will Rogers; and a spoiled-rotten Valley Girl. On the morning of the actual performance, the raw talent oozing from our prodigies was almost palpable.

Once the comedy was over, the children wound down and we moved to a more serious scene. Heather, the oldest female of the grandkids, carried out a Christmas tradition from Sweden. Wearing a long-skirted Christmas dress, her hair wreathed with a garland, she sang "Silent Night" for her family audience. We discussed decorating the garland in her hair with lighted candles, but my reputation for setting hair afire at Christmas gatherings kept us in check.

Following Heather's solo, Rachel Praise and Cousin Hartley joined in with a great rendition of "Away in a Manger." Then it fell to Scott, the Freeman Christmas storyteller, to come up with an authentic sounding tale about a special Christmas in the Old Country. He didn't disappoint us, coming out in rare form with accents and gestures and facial expressions that held the children spellbound.

After the show, we gathered around the festive table where Jim thanked the Lord for keeping us together as a family, and for the greatest gift of all—His Son. For the grand finale, we dived into a scrumptious smorgasbord of Swedish meatballs with all the trimmings.

On the first Easter after Scott and I were married, my mother gave us a copy of *What Is a Family?* by Edith Schaeffer. It's been one of the most significant books I've read and it has continued to shape my own desire to put my family at the top of my life's priorities, difficult as that is in these hectic times in which we live. I've referred to Mrs. Schaeffer's writing again and again over the years, with so many sentences marked that—in the tradition of my father—practically the entire book is underlined. One of my favorite chapters is entitled "A Museum of Memories."

Mrs. Schaeffer believes that every family deposits memories into the family museum—some good, some painful. In the case of my own little family, my parents, and my in-laws, we have all—on various occasions—deposited both kinds. But even the bad memories, when looked at in a certain light, can be redeemed.

As a young bride coping with some of the inevitable disillusionments of marriage—scared to death that every conflict might turn into the memory that would forever end our relationship—Edith's words of honesty and wisdom gave me perspective and the will to help pick up the broken pieces and, with Scott's help, start over again and again. Eighteen years later, we're still in the process of blowing it and making fresh starts. And every time the pieces are back in place, I think to myself, *Yep, this relationship stuff can be exhausting. But it is so good to be close again, and, yes, it is worth it.*

There is no family who has a picture perfect museum of memories, of course, but I want to encourage myself and others to continue making deliberate efforts, even at the sacrifice of time and energy, to use some of the time we have left on this earth to fill our family's museum with wonderful, happy memories.

Memories aren't just events that happen once and disappear into the atmosphere. They are embedded in the backs of our minds, affecting how we function, think, feel, and make decisions. How very thankful I am to both sets of my children's grandparents for purposefully, often sacrificially, making it a priority to create good memories for their adult children and grandkids.

As in the case of my husband's mother, Beverly, I personally hope that her efforts in making fun memories will always take precedence over old, dull housekeeping. Besides, I agree wholeheartedly with the words I saw at the mall recently, written on a lavender T-shirt worn by a modern granny—"Housework makes you ugly." For what will the family most remember? A perfectly scrubbed home—or a *museum of memories?*

An empty stable stays clean—but there is no income from an empty stable.

PROVERBS 14:4, TLB

A Cartridge
in a Bear Tree

It's bedtime, 1968. A boy, age eleven, lies on the bottom bunk trying desperately to fall asleep. Unfortunately the occupant of the top bunk is Scott—age ten. He is hanging his head over his perch, eyes wide open in a zombielike stare, patiently peering down at his big brother for the sheer pleasure of brotherly aggravation. To the "stare-ee" it's like the slow drip of Chinese water torture. And finally, Kent, the boy on the bottom, explodes.

"I can't take it anymore! Scott, go to sleep!!!"

Scott, delighted to have finally caught his brother's attention, launches into his second favorite nocturnal game: last word. Both boys go at it, each determined to say the last sentence before they fall asleep. Scott may be the youngest; he may be the shortest; he may also be the most immature. But he also possesses endurance beyond comprehension, and to Kent's intense irritation Scott always wins the game. When Kent is somewhere between consciousness and the inevitable pull of deep and overwhelming sleep, he faintly hears Scott mumble with his last ounce of strength, "Word."

And so went the brotherly game, night after night, year after year with Scott always getting in the last "word." Until I entered the picture. I am the Undisputed Champion of Nighttime Talking, and when Scott married me, he found he had finally met his match.

If I were to take you by the hand and lead you on a tour through the branches of the Freeman family tree, you would notice an interesting pattern among the males. In the last three generations, there are several sets of brothers, less than two years apart. In my in-law's photo gallery rests an old cracked and faded photo of Scott's father, Jim, and Jim's younger brother, Lee. It's impossible not to notice that Jim and Lee are mirror images of Kent and Scott.

Even more strange is the fact that Scott married me, a short brunette named Becky, and our first two sons, Zach and Zeke, are eighteen months apart. Kent, Scott's big brother, also married a short brunette named Becky, and they have two sons, Clint and Blake, who are equally close in age. It's eerie.

Back in the lean postdepression years when Jim and Lee were kids, they had also been great buddies. They were both raised to work hard on the family farm—so hard in fact that Jim grew up with no romantic ideas about life among cows and cornfields. But when Jim reminisces about the "olden days," he also recalls some halcyon summer afternoons, once the chores were done. It was then that he and his brother, Lee, would steal off to go fishing and swimming together in a nearby lake.

Today Jim's adult children have also become fishing buddies of a different sort. Now Scott and Kent and their sister, Laura—the thirty-something siblings—go on special deep sea fishing trips together—no parents, spouses, or kids invited. It warms my heart to observe how the three of them have remained good friends, each of them taking the initiative to call the other one just to see how things are going. Since my own brother and sister live across the country, I've especially appreciated my friendship with Scott's siblings, Kent and Laura, who live much closer.

In talking with Laura recently, I discovered an interesting fact I hadn't known before. She told me in a quiet moment that even though she is the oldest child, she's always looked up to Kent as if he were her big brother. Actually, Kent's six-foot-plus frame requires that most people look up to him.

Kent is a real live working cowboy, long and lean, and when you add a wide-brimmed cowboy hat, I'm talking *tall!* Complete the picture with a handlebar mustache so impressive that it curls around and completely covers his upper lip—and I'm talking *impressive!* He almost seems to be a man from another time—when men were real men and ruled the West with sheer grit, very few words, and plenty of hard labor. Not what you'd call the sentimental type.

Though a man's man, Kent has always been kind, especially to Scott. He never treated him like a pesky tag-a-long kid brother, even during the teenage years when image is everything. As a result, even though Scott had a different personality from Kent's, he always admired him. When other people notice Kent as he ambles into a room—all six-foot-two inches of blue jeans, bow legs, and bull skin boots, not to mention the inches added by his Stetson hat—I've heard Scott say with quiet pride, "That's my brother."

The first time I remember seeing Kent, I was thirteen and we were at church camp. After the evening service I found him sitting in the middle of a group of junior high and high school kids giving an impromptu demonstration with a candy bar. Actually, he was pretending to be committing hara-kiri by slowly pulling on the caramel center which represented—ingeniously, I thought—intestines. He must have been about fifteen at the time.

Later that evening, out in a gazebo under the stars, he did an on-the-spot ventriloquist routine using a large, deceased bull-frog for a dummy. It goes without saying that his performances commanded the respect of his audience, which happened to include both me and Scott. The next morning Kent gave me, the new kid at camp, a real Texas welcome by unloading a gallon bucket of a seaweedy lake grunge on my head.

In another prime example from days gone by, Kent and his high school buddy, Steve, along with three girls from church, "kidnapped" a mutual friend, Karen, on her sixteenth birthday. Trying to come up with a truly meaningful memory for Karen's special day, the group decided to take her to the newly opened Dallas/Ft. Worth airport for a midnight stroll.

Kent and Steve had observed that the DFW Airport was usually filled with fascinating characters from near and far, especially during the seventies. People hardly turned for a second look at bald monks wearing saffron robes or suburban women returning from island vacations with gigantic fruit topped hats. Hardly more did they turn to stare at men wearing the same garb. The two birthday hosts felt really challenged to see if they could come up with something that might actually turn heads at the airport.

As I understand it, Steve devised a plan which first involved wrapping Kent from head to toe in aluminum foil. (Why ask why?) Then Steve, dressed in jean cutoffs and cowboy boots led Kent, the Tin Foil Man, on a leash through the airport accompanied by their entourage of teenage girls. I hear they raised a few eyebrows, but no one in the people-watching paradise seemed unduly alarmed or even particularly surprised. Such was the seventies, and such was my future brother-in-law.

After Scott and I married, we were concerned about Kent finding just the right wife. We both knew it would take someone special to appreciate his finer points—the ability to look cool while dressed in tin foil and communicating via candy bars, bull frogs, and seaweed. She had to be of hearty stock to complement Kent's dream of going into the horse business and/or ranching. In addition, she'd have to be pretty, or Kent would probably never look twice. Being a matchmaker at heart, I looked far and wide for a suitable mate for Kent. Then one day I thought of Becky Kemp, an adorable friend of mine from high school whose dad had been in the horse business for years. She'd be perfect!

Scott and I drove up to the ranch where Kent was working while he attended college, and I couldn't wait to tell my new brother-in-law that I had found *the* girl for him.

"Kent, " I began almost as soon as I fell out of the car, "have I got the *perfect* girl for you. Now you may think she's a little young, but she's really cute, and she knows how to handle horses and . . . ."

"Yep," Kent drawled, "already asked her to marry me."

Well, you could have knocked me over with a quail feather, and Kent enjoyed watching every minute of it. He'd beaten me to the punch, but I'll say this for him. The man has good taste, but it presented the Freeman family with a small problem. They now had two family members named Becky Freeman. So the two of us became Kent's Becky and Scott's Becky. I know—it's hard to believe that this neck of the woods can survive more than one Becky Freeman, isn't it?

The *new* Becky Freeman was tailor-made for her husband and he for her. And they had their own special way of communicating, too. During their courtship and after they were first married, one of the main ways they showed affection was to tickle, chase, and playfully wrestle with each other. To them, there was nothing quite as romantic as one catching the other in a gripping head lock and holding the other just to see how long it could be maintained. It was touching to behold.

Not only does my sister-in-law have a terrific sense of humor, but she does indeed know about horses and tack and auctions and cow stuff. She also plays a mean game of volleyball alongside Kent on their city's volleyball team. I'm very much in awe of this. I, at age thirty-five, have never been able to serve a volleyball over the net without receiving massive bruises to the delicate tissues on my forearm.

In numerous ways, I've grown to admire Kent's Becky more with each passing year. She's wise, good, stable, and bighearted;

and most important of all—she has the ability to handle macho men with hardly more than a raised eyebrow.

Scott is also of the macho variety, to a point—it simply can't be helped within the Freeman male bloodline. He is tall, muscular, and strong. Our children obey his soft-spoken requests the moment he speaks, not out of fear but out of respect. And Scott's as stubborn as a mule in an argument with me, but not too far beneath the surface is a tender and romantic man. We each can't believe we have found in the other someone to satisfy our unusual penchants for long, deep talks over the meaning of life—often over morning cups of coffee. Or sometimes at sunset. On many a clear night, one can find Scott philosophizing into the wee hours with me out under the stars. Even some of our neighbors join in our late-night, lakeside roundtable.

Having scientifically observed a few sets of brothers, I've come to this conclusion: There is an invisible barrier and an equally invisible bond between brothers who are close in age. There are times I think that my own two oldest boys, Zach and Zeke, are inseparable. They share a room, friends, activities, and fun. They take up for each other at school. Then there are times they seem so different, I can hardly believe they share the same set of biological parents. It's as if the boys purposely choose to excel at different sports, subjects, and interests just to keep their own precious identities intact.

So it appears to be with Scott and Kent even now when I contemplate these two brothers. Sometimes I think of the two characters from the TV mini-series, *Lonesome Dove*. Captain Call reminds me of Kent in many ways. The good captain was a courageous man and a loyal friend, but he had the dickens of a time saying anything that might be misconstrued as sentimental mush—even to those closest to him. To his credit, however, Captain Call always managed to hold on to his honor, and the people around him were loyal to him to their dying breath.

Then there was Augustus, or "Gus," in whose character I can see so much of Scott. Gus was tough as nails when it came to fightin' the Indians, and he was highly respected by men, but get him around a pretty woman and he—how do I describe this?—well, he sort of melted all over. When a lady was hurt, either physically or emotionally, ol' Gus knew instinctively how to comfort her. Gus's gentleness toward the womenfolk got him in a few jams, but his tender heart endeared his character to thousands of readers and viewers. As for me, I realize that I need a Gus. One disclaimer here: I prefer my dream Gus stick to one woman. Otherwise, he might get to be a genuine Lonesome Dove.

Though Scott and Kent are not exactly the same under the skin, they are looking more alike on the surface with each passing year. This spring, Kent came out to join Scott and his dad as they put a roof on our house. I marveled at how much Scott and Kent are metamorphosing in their old age, into the image of their father. They stroke their chins, have a habit of sniffing while scrunching their noses off to one side, walk with one leg slightly bowed, and grab their backs when they get up out of chairs. Need to know how the world of politics functions? Ask Scott, Kent, or Jim. They've had the topic tied up neatly in a red-necked bandanna for years. Still, the three of them make a trio of good lookin', hard-workin', rugged, helpful, faithful men—the kind that single women wish had extra brothers to go around.

Anyway, after a few hours of swinging hammers and cutting lumber that warm afternoon of working on the roof, Scott came in the house and thirstily downed a glass of ice water. He paused for a second, set the glass firmly down on the counter, wiped his mouth with the back of his hand, looked me straight in the eyes, and said, "Beck, we've still got it."

"Got what?" I asked. Then it dawned on me. Kent and Scott had been in the construction business together a few years back. Eventually, Kent saddled up and chose to ride the trail leading to ranch management, and Scott donned an executive suit and drove though Dallas traffic to his position in facility/property management. But back when the Freeman brothers worked side by side, they had made quite the team.

"Kent knows precisely where I want a board," Scott continued, "and I know what he needs me to saw next, without our ever having to say a word. It's like we know exactly what each other is thinking."

I winked in Scott's direction, leaned across the kitchen counter, put my hand on his arm and said, "Maybe you two *are* related."

Looking back, they often had made a good team. One of Scott's best memories of Kent as a child is the hours they spent playing army men. Long afternoons were often filled with making intricate forts out of dirt, sticks, and grass and preparing strategy plans for attack and defense with a bucket full of army-green plastic figures.

Years later, as teenagers, they were comrades in games of capture the flag with the Boys' Brigade from church. Kent and Scott were a great team—one diverting the attention of the guard, while the other pulled the famous sneak attack and grabbed the flag. With Kent's high jumping athletic ability and Scott's muscular build and gymnastic skills, they were practically unbeatable.

Yesterday, the dynamic duo, Rambo Kent and G.I. Scott, got to relive that memory. Scott, Zach, and Zeke joined Uncle Kent and cousins, Clint and Blake, along with several teenagers, to celebrate Zeke's thirteenth birthday. They did so by participating in a pseudomilitary game called paint ball wars, the newest brain child of some enterprising entrepreneurs for which our clever warriors paid real money.

They camped out in dusty, mosquito-infested woods on Friday night and then awakened Saturday morning, eager for battle. They dressed out in protective head gear and were issued high-powered guns filled with bullets of orange, white, and yellow paint. Scott and Kent transformed into big army generals, each leading opposing troops of teenage mutant soldiers.

The "generals" seriously strategized their attack and defense plans, going over the famous "divert and strike ploy" with their army of wide-eyed, clueless thirteen- and fourteen-year-old draftees. After the war, it was evident from the multiple paint ball bruises on Scott's and Kent's bodies that their troops could have used some boot camp training.

When the men arrived home, they were covered with dirt and paint and dazed with exhaustion, proving once again that war is "you know what." The boys headed straight to the bedroom and collapsed. Scott and Kent stopped briefly at the kitchen counter where I was on K.P. duty, making hot dogs for the pitiful, half-starved stragglers. Scott found his voice first.

"Becky," he managed, and the voice cracked, "I led those boys in a sneak attack. I told 'em I'd go in first. Draw the fire and cover for 'em. Then they were to run in behind me and go for the flag. (Here, he shook his downcast head.) Well, I ran into the field, and before I knew what hit me, I was ambushed with paint balls from every side, sacrificing myself for the sake of my troops. Where were those boys? *They were crouched behind a barricade like a bunch of yellow bellied recruits!*

"What was the deal?!?" I asked them.

From somewhere deep in their bedroom came one last feeble protest. "But, Dad! They were shooting at us!"

"Man," Uncle Kent joined in, shaking his head, "what's the matter with these kids today! Whatever happened to 'death before dishonor'?"

As Kent complained, Scott eased his body gingerly onto the couch. "Miss Becky?" he asked in a little boy voice, "Um, could you bring me a pillow, please, ma'm?"

"Well, you bet, sweety," I answered. "Anything for my big, strong army man."

About that time, Kent found his way to the recliner, barely able to find the strength to pull the lever to bring up the footrest. Within minutes, the only sound I heard issuing from the living room was two low-pitched snores. It was a pitiful sight, really.

More than three sets of visitors came and went throughout the afternoon without either brother having the slightest idea of their presence.

As I watched Kent and Scott sleep and shushed the people walking in and out of the house, I felt a strange motherly twinge. I found myself thinking, *They must have been pretty cute little tikes when they were kids—individuals, yes, but unmistakably brothers.*

With the years came inevitable changes. The brothers no longer sleep on bunks or live in the same house anymore. Scott no longer has the energy to outlast Kent when it comes to staying awake, and yet there was a sense of 1968 nostalgia in my living-room-turned-sleeping-quarters. I looked at Scott—his eyes closed and his mouth open, then at Kent—conked out, only his mustache moving slightly under his breath. From my position in the kitchen—like the proverbial fly on the wall—I watched the scene, smiled in victory, and quietly whispered, "Word."

Whoever loves his brother lives in the light.

1 JOHN 2:10, NIV

A Yellow Bird Afraid of
One Little Swallow

Today is the seventh of July, three days after the fireworks exploded over our nation and our lakeside cabin. On most Fourths of July the Freeman clan gathers at our place. Years ago we established our holiday plan. Jim and Beverly would host Christmas as only Beverly can do—with lots of new recipes gleaned from her *Creative Cooking* magazines; Kent and Becky would do Thanksgiving with the turkey and her special sage and cornbread stuffing; Laura would play hostess at Easter with her wonderful baked ham and homemade candies. And I? I was assigned the Fourth of July because there was not a lot of damage I could do to a hot dog.

This year, for reasons of vacationing and conflicting plans, only Scott's sister, Laura, and her daughters, Heather and Hartley came out to join us. Scott and Laura and I lay in the sun on the deck like roast chickens turning on a spit.

As the three of us baked, we also enjoyed cool drinks and—with nothing on our agenda for the long afternoon but relaxing and relating—we waxed philosophical. As we discussed the process of becoming grown-up adults, each of us in some personal sphere declared our independence. It just seemed appropriate to the occasion.

As we were heavy into one profound topic after another, my little nine-year-old niece Hartley strolled up to join us. She looked as cute as a button in her new haircut and pierced ears, and I pointed this out to her. Always up for a conversation, she dove right in.

"Thank you, Aunt Becky. Some of the kids said my hair made me look like a boy. It really bothered Heather." I wondered if in reality it bothered Hartley more. "Well, darlin'," I asked my niece, "Did it hurt your feelings, too?"

Quite matter of factly, she stated, "Oh, I'm OK with it. It just made Heather really mad."

I crooked my finger toward Hartley, motioning for her to come near me for a hug. She's such a sweetheart, and it touched me to see her more concerned about her sister's reaction than the fact that she had been the object of mean-spirited teasing.

"Now tell me about getting your ears pierced, Hartley," I suggested. Delighted to have the attention of an adult, Hartley launched into her tale.

"Well, the first time I ever got my ear pierced it was by my friend's ferret," she began. My eyebrows may have shot up a little because she hurried to explain.

"See, I was petting the ferret, and then all of the sudden it bit right through my ear. Well, Heather saw me screaming and turnin' sick, and she took a great big ol' baseball bat and just knocked that ferret right off my ear."

Realizing we were on to something here, I ran inside for a pad and pencil then rejoined the roasters and my niece. I didn't want to miss a word.

Settling into her story, Hartley continued as I took dictation. "Then the next time I had my ears pierced it was by this lady at the mall, and she must have petted dirty animals or gotten into some pest control stuff or something because my ear got germs all stuck inside the hole; by the time we got to the doctor my ear lobe was so big it nearly exploded off my head."

I glanced over at Laura who just shrugged her shoulders and nodded. There was more. Hartley's bright eyes danced with her most recent ear-piercing excitement.

"This time for my birthday, we went to a lady at a store who wore clean gloves, and everything went just fine except for I fainted, and Heather and Dad had to carry me over and lay me on a bench, and the security guard had to come and write all about it in case we wanted to sue anybody."

So you've met Hartley. Her big sister, Heather, is also a case all her own. She was currently lolling on the grass with the other kids, so I called to her and she strolled over from the grass to the deck.

Heather is eleven, with the face and figure of a fifteen-year-old model, but she's anything but a delicate flower. With pencil poised I asked her to tell me about the time she confronted the rat. I'd heard the story before, but now seemed like a good time to get the fine details.

"Well, let me think," she began as she stretched her long legs to catch a few rays. "I guess I was about seven, and I went outside and saw my cat rasslin' with a rat. Now this rat was almost as big as the cat—at least a foot long without its tail. I was afraid my cat might lose the fight so I decided to help her kill the rat. I made a fist to try to knock the rat unconscious, but when I did that it bit into my hand. I raised up and flung that rat as far as I could throw it, and my cat finally got her dinner."

Wide-eyed, I asked the obvious questions. "Did you cry? Were you scared? Did you tell your mom?"

"Nope," Heather answered matter-of-factly, "But when I got in the house and started doctoring myself up in the bathroom, Momma yelled, 'Heather, what happened?' She always knows these things somehow. When I told her it was just a rat bite, she called the health department right away. That's when the trouble really started."

How well I remembered that time. Week after week, since the rat only existed in the form of digested cat food, Heather—heroine and defender of the felines—had to go for the awful series of rabies shots. There was nothing funny about that part of the story.

Laura, Laura, Laura, I thought, *You've raised some interesting children.*

Laura's girls were so obviously independent that I wondered about Laura herself. Her reputation for being a less than docile teenager was well documented. However she was, she is now a dedicated teacher for young children in a special education classroom and has turned her energy toward motivating these special kids day after day.

While I had Laura "on the couch," I sat up in a lawn chair, crossed my legs, and tapped my pencil on my pad of paper. In the voice of a famous German psychiatrist I said, "OK, Laura. Let's talk about you. Vat are some constructive vays you've found to be unique, to separate your identity from that of your parents? Vy don't you begin by telling me about your animals. I understand you have a few, ya?"

Laura perked up at one of her favorite topics. Her father, Jim, had often said that the only animal he ever wanted was one that could live on gasoline and would turn off when he clicked a key. Laura had declared her independence by taking a different view of nature's friends.

She seemed at a loss for where to begin so I suggested that she simply start by listing the animals that she currently owns, and I would write them down.

"All right," Laura began, "Let's start with the dogs. There's the collie, Rosie. Then there's Idiot Dog."

At this point Hartley interjected, "Yeah, he always bites us on the behind when we walk outside."

I smiled as Laura continued her itemization. "Then there's the poor excuse for a dog—Misty Boo-Boo, our Yorkshire terrier. And the four Siamese cats. We also have a flat nose

Persian with a stuck-up chin, the kind you see in prissy elegant cat commercials—only ours is missing a tail that she lost in a not-so-elegant fight.

"Then there is our sable ferret, Tessa, who attacks our feet and likes to root under the sheets in our bed. She's great. There's the two iguanas—Wild Thing and Rocky. The turtle we call Dude and the tarantula. Of course, there are our gerbils which were actually bought for animal food, but the girls got attached to them before I could feed them to Elizabeth."

"Elizabeth?" I asked, hopeful that the entity belonging to that very innocent-sounding name was something less than human.

"Oh, yes. Have I not told you about Elizabeth and Charles, our two ball pythons?"

"Elizabeth isn't the 'secret animal' you lost in the house for three weeks?"

"As a matter-of-fact, she is. I was washing the clothes when I put my hand down around the bottom of the tub and felt something like a belt, only fatter. I had no idea how many cycles she'd been through, but she sure smelled clean."

I shivered, but analysts must not be faint of heart. Besides, this was beginning to sound intriguing. I could almost see a headline: Dr. DooLaura Caught in Snake Laundering Scandal.

"Anything else you vant to get off your shest, Dahlink?" I asked.

"Oh, I almost forgot. There's my baby, my red-tipped boa named Sheila. And, of course, Heather's albino Burmese python, Teila."

"Laura," I asked, forgetting about the accent, "just out of curiosity, how large will these snakes get?"

"Oh, around eighteen feet long and about twelve inches around."

"Laura," I said, abandoning all attempts at detachment, "I think it is wise that you've talked all of this animal fixation stuff out of your system. Confession is good for the soul, but as your friend and sister-in-law and amateur shrink, I think I need to gently say a few guiding words about your newfound independence: It seems to me that you have developed a terrible case of obsessive-compulsive disorder accompanied by neurosis of the liver with symptoms of hysterical schizophrenic psychotic dementia."

Laura looked at me as if *I* needed a straightjacket. I could see that being tactful was getting me nowhere. So I tried an alternate therapeutic approach.

"Let's see if I can put this another way: Laura!!! You're not living in a house. You're living in an ark! Wake up and smell the cobra!!! We are talking about man-killing snakes here bigger than my station wagon! Are you *nuts?*"

"No," Laura yawned as she stretched, "I'm just unique."

How could I argue with that? It was Laura's home, Laura's choice, Laura's life. After all, hadn't we all just declared our independence from meeting up to others' expectations?

"OK, Laura, it's your decision, but I'm just warning you. When those things get as big as fire hoses, I'm not bringing my children or small dogs to your house."

Laura seemed to understand my feelings, but she was determined to keep her menagerie and actually add to her collection. When we took the girls shopping that afternoon, she bought a luxury heating pad *for the snakes!* Before she packed to go home the next day, we visited again. I steered the conversation away from the subject of animals.

"So, what are you going to do with your week, Laura?" I asked.

"I'm going shopping for a hedgehog," she joked. So much for subject steering.

I laughed out loud at the thought of it. "Why not? All you need is a hog, right? Miss Piggy with a spike hair-do!"

Guess what? She wasn't joking.

I just got the happy announcement via telephone: I've been made an auntie again—to a baby porcupine hog critter the size of a baseball who goes by the name of Sonic. Of course, Sonic has to be handled with leather gloves, but he's "just the most adorable thing you ever saw." Not only that, but Sonic is getting a girlfriend next week so the two of them can fall in love when they grow up and get married and have lots and lots of little expensive prickly hog babies.

Whoops, the phone just rang again. It was Laura. "Did I mention that we also brought home a dwarf Siamese bunny and a black mother bunny with six babies? But you can relax, Becky. A lot of these pets will live in my classroom during the school year, and give some really special kids a lot of pleasure. They're going to be thrilled."

I'm sure they will, Laura. It takes a special person to teach special kids, and you are that. I hope all the animals have at least one baby apiece for the kids to love. Noah would be proud.

Bring out every kind of living creature that is with you—the birds, the animals, and all the creatures that move along the ground—so they can multiply on the earth and be fruitful and increase in number upon it.

GENESIS 8:17, NIV

PART FIVE

Tremors Hit the Treetops

A Tree
Shaken to Its Roots

The second half of the year 1986 was the sort of year one doesn't easily forget. Or ever want to live through again. My family and my extended family experienced just about all the possible major events a family can have—births, deaths, marriages, moves, closing up my Nonnie's homeplace, etc. etc. For starters, Mother and Daddy made their second cross-country move, back to Texas from Virginia, just in time to take over the primary responsibility for Nonnie, who was quickly losing her bout with time. So were both Grandmother and Granddaddy Arnold, for that matter, but Uncle Buddy and Aunt Hazel seemed to have that situation under control.

In October, Gabriel joined our family tree, and Mother ran our household for a week, giving me time to begin the adjustment to four children. I had exactly one month to complete this little transition before we all converged on Virginia for my sister Rachel's wedding to Scott St. John-Gilbert. Somewhere between birthin' babies and chasing Nonnie in the night, Mother had managed to make the bride's gown, not to mention one of the dresses for the matrons of honor (me), the flower girl (Rachel

Praise), and small suits for the two ringbearers (Zach and Zeke). Lazy thing, she had not gotten all the drapes made for her new house before heading back to Virginia, two weeks ahead of Daddy to help prepare for the wedding. He remained behind in his new and unfamiliar abode, wondering who was staring in through the undraped windows at him each night.

During those weeks, Grandmother Arnold escaped from her Alzheimer's prison, dying peacefully in her sleep. A few months later, it became apparent that Nonnie could no longer live in her home out in West Texas without a relative in her small town to look after her. Longtime friends and a paid attendant had done the best they could, but Nonnie was losing her hold on reality. She insisted on getting up about every thirty to forty-five minutes at night to make her way to the bathroom and, at least once a night, fell and bruised or cut herself in new places. Mother and her five siblings concurred. Nonnie would move in with her. That was the way Mother wanted it.

One morning a few weeks after the move, it dawned on me that I had not been seeing much of my mother of late. I knew she was looking after Nonnie, but still, it was only an hour and a half drive to my house. . . . I decided to give her a call.

"I miss you, too," she assured me. "But last night was the twenty-fourth night I have slept in the twin bed beside Nonnie, getting up with her five and six times a night to make sure she doesn't fall when she goes to the bathroom."

"Congratulations!" I commiserated. "Sounds like you've become a card-carrying member of the sandwich generation."

"That's putting it mildly. Don't they have a sandwich up North they call a grinder?"

"I've always thought of you more as spicy ham and rye," I responded. "Are we ever going to see you again? Is there any way I can help?"

"Unfortunately, honey, I don't think there is. You have your own hands full, and the saddest thing of all is, your four little ones just wouldn't mix very well with Nonnie at this stage. She is *so* fragile and unsteady on her feet. I'm beginning to see that there's not going to be much of a normal life for me—or for Daddy—if I try to keep Nonnie here with us.

"The one night I tried sleeping in my own bed, I heard her bumping around in the night and found her wandering in the family room. She seems to be more disoriented at night, and neither of us are getting any rest. I can hardly stand it, but it looks like we may have to put her into a nursing home."

I felt my stomach wrench. *Can this be happening?* I wondered. *My Nonnie? Nursing home? This happens to other people.* "Can't you hire someone to stay with her at night?" I asked.

"Nonnie has almost no money of her own, and the only government aid we can get is if she needed a visiting nurse to bathe her and check her medically each day—which she doesn't need. I am more than happy to bathe her, and her medications are fairly simple. What we need are sitters so I can get away for a few hours and someone to look after her at night. But that would eat up every cent of her savings within two or three months and far exceed her monthly social security checks thereafter. This comes at a time when we have to be saving for our own retirement years to avoid being a burden to *our* kids. It's ironic, but if we put Nonnie in a nursing home, the government takes over completely, even though the cost of her care there would be a lot more than the cost of her care here with us."

"I am *so* sorry." I genuinely felt for both Mother and Nonnie—and a little sorry for myself and my kids. I knew how much my mother loved her mother and how much she had wanted to take care of her in her old age. Apparently we were both just now realizing the cost. "Now what?" I asked.

"I've talked to all the others in the family, and they're in agreement that we have reached the end of our capacity to care for Nonnie ourselves—except for your Uncle J. R. and Aunt Martha. She wants to give it one more try at her home. So . . .

we plan to bundle Nonnie into the van and try to make the trip to Houston."

"Do you think Nonnie can stand the trip?" I asked.

"I *think* so. She actually seems a little stronger physically and steadier on her feet since she came here. But I think we'll go as far as Belton and spend the night with your Uncle Lloyd. That will break the trip up, and since he's a doctor, I feel better about stopping there for the night." It sounded like a good plan, until I heard from Mother once they reached Houston.

"You're not going to believe this one!" she said on the other end of the wire, but she was laughing, so it was a good sign. "We got to Uncle Lloyd's, and I told him I hadn't had a full night's sleep in over three weeks, and it had been longer than that for Nonnie.

"'Well,' he said in his best doctor tone, 'I'll fix that!' So at bedtime, he brought out a sleeping pill—a huge, bright red gel cap that looked like it could put a horse to bed for a month. She swallowed it like a good girl, and we sat for a minute or two at the table saying goodnight to Lloyd, and then I took her into the bathroom to get her ready for bed. I helped her undress and then cleaned her bridge work and gave her a toothbrush to brush what was left of her own teeth.

"She bent over the sink, and the first thing I knew, she started to sway. I grabbed her and started leading her out of the bathroom, hoping I could get her to the bed before she fell sound asleep. I could tell within a few steps we weren't going to make it. By the time I yelled for Uncle Lloyd and we struggled with her to the nearest chair, we were sweating profusely, and she was snoring soundly!

"I told Lloyd as we huffed and puffed and got her into bed, 'This is one night it looks like I'm going to get some rest!'

"Little did I know! At 2:00 A.M., Nonnie rose off her pillow like some filmy apparition, determined to get up, and go to the bathroom. She was just groggy enough to be *really* unsteady on her feet, so I had to yell for Uncle Lloyd to help me take her.

We managed to get her back to bed, and she did go back to sleep without getting up again, but by 7:00 the next morning, she was far wider awake than I was!

"She made the trip the rest of the way to Houston just great. Me? I was out on my feet!"

In Houston, a nephew who was also a doctor, suggested Nonnie's mental problems just might be caused by a lack of vitamin B12 and started her on monthly injections. Amazingly, more of the real Nonnie began to come back to us. Whether it was the B12, or the stimulation of being in Houston with more of her family about her, we'll never know, but Nonnie's mind began to be much clearer, and she became more stable as she walked. In just a few weeks, she was getting up only a couple of times at night and taking care of her own needs when she did. The family let out a huge, collective sigh of relief and then devised a visitation system in which Nonnie lived among four of her children for six weeks at a time.

This continued for eighteen months. It wasn't perfect, by any means, but we were all determined, if at all possible, that Nonnie would live out her days cared for by her family. Mother made her dresses—pretty pastels that were easy to get into, and both her daughters and daughters-in-law could comb her lovely silver hair into a most becoming French twist. She spent her days quietly sitting in the living room rocker, her hands folded in her lap, her soft blue eyes gazing into the past. Every now and then she would give herself a mental health check up.

"Cantaloupe," she would say quietly. "C-a-n-t-a-l-o-u-p-e." Then she would look at Mother and give her a beaming look of triumph, as if to say, "If I can still spell cantaloupe, I must be OK!"

But the day finally came when Nonnie, age eighty-five, was not OK. She suffered a stroke during one of her six-week stays at Uncle Genie's in Houston. Mother flew down to be with her in the hospital and called regularly to give me reports.

"She has no physical paralysis, but her mind is thoroughly scrambled. She's as giddy as a school girl! Wouldn't that mortify her if she knew? She's still well able to pop out of the bed but not able to stay on her feet for sure or to know where she's going once she's *on* her feet. So, I'm staying with her day and night here in the hospital."

"Are you getting any rest?" I asked.

"Enough. I have a cot by her bed, but she doesn't sleep much and doesn't like for me to. Last night when I tried to sleep, she'd gather up her sheet and form a long piece of it. Then she'd draw back like a teenage boy in a locker room and try to *pop* me with it to wake me up!" The mental picture of my genteel little Nonnie trying to towel pop my mother was so incredible we both had to laugh. In times like these, you take humor where you can get it. A few days later Mother called me, chuckling again.

"Yesterday a physical therapist came in to see Nonnie. I'm sure he wanted to see if she'd suffered any muscular damage from the stroke. Wouldn't you know he'd be tall, dark, and handsome! The minute he walked in the door, Nonnie looked up and said, 'Bob Wheeler!'

"I *knew* she had mistaken him for her young preacher from back home and thought he had come all that way to see her. Talk about thrilled! Then he walked to her bed and took her hand, and she gazed up at him with pure rapture. Being a therapist and *not* a preacher, he began to gently move her arm up and down, which I'm sure she saw as just a sweet gesture as he talked with her about how she was feeling.

"All went well until he asked her, 'Mrs. Jones, do you mind if I look at your leg?' The expression on her face was so shocked, I had to try hard to keep from guffawing. Talk about disapproving! After a long minute, she looked up at him with a frown that would have frozen the Sahara."

"'I guess not,' she finally managed to say, *very* coldly. 'It'll hurt you worse'n it'll hurt me!'"

It *was* funny, but by the time Nonnie was ready to be released, nothing was funny about what the doctor told the family. "I don't believe you will be able to keep her in your homes anymore. She is now incontinent, her mind is probably never going to be normal again, yet she is so very ambulatory. She will have to be either restrained or watched constantly. The burden will be intolerable."

And so the period began that Mother has referred to as the hardest in her life. The family tried a nursing home in Houston, and the first time Mother went to see Nonnie, she understood fully why so many people feel such guilt about placing their loved ones in institutions. She found Nonnie restrained and lying in her own filth, her lovely silver hair drawn into a tiny, ugly knot on top of her head. Attendants ignored the buzzer on the side of Nonnie's bed and ignored Mother when she went to the front desk and asked for help. She wondered if anybody noticed the day she marched in and wheeled Nonnie out of the place, stopping just long enough to notify the front desk. Mother finally took Nonnie back to her hometown where she hoped she could find a facility close enough to her own house so she could keep closer watch on her.

Within three weeks at the second facility, Nonnie had ulcerated legs from being restrained in a wheel chair with her feet dangling for too long. On the morning she found Nonnie lying in her filth once again, on wet sheets with an air conditioner blowing on her, she found a wheel chair and took her home *before* notifying the front desk.

She had come full circle. The marathon nights began again, with Mother trying to persuade Nonnie to stay in bed. The first three mornings, Mother changed the soaked sheets before sending Daddy to buy adult diapers. On the fifth morning after she had spent another sleepless night trying to keep Nonnie in bed, she sadly bought a restrainer, and that night slipped the jacket with the very long ties on Nonnie, who didn't seem to notice. Mother made sure that Nonnie had gone to the bathroom and had had a drink of water, and then tied the ties to the bed rails. She then lay down on the couch in the living room to see how it would go.

"I need to go to the bathroom," Nonnie called first. From the couch, Mother called back.

"I just took you to the bathroom, honey. Try to go to sleep." There was a long silence, and Mother almost dropped off to sleep. Then she heard Nonnie call to her again.

"Just a cold drink of water would taste awfully good."

The role reversal was now complete. Mother knew in that moment that she was attempting the impossible. There was no family member to help closer than two hundred miles, and there would be no family life of any other kind with Nonnie requiring this kind of care. Was it fair to Daddy? Was it fair to her grandchildren? And it would not be fair to any of her siblings to ask them to do what she could not do. They all had the same considerations she had. But what an awful choice to have to make!

The next day she hired a sitter through a sitting service and went out to inquire as to the very best nursing home in the area. She then made an appointment at the beauty salon to do the unthinkable—to have Nonnie's long silver hair "bobbed" and curled, hoping to avoid that ugly little knot at the top of her head once she would be in the nursing home. Nonnie seemed not to notice, but it made the rest of us feel better to see our Nonnie's beautiful hair looking pretty. Immediately after the appointment, she drove her to the nursing home. It was then that Nonnie began to notice her surroundings.

Within a week, she had lost all her sense of dignity and yelled at the top of her lungs. Within two months she was bedfast, her limbs useless from being restrained and without any therapy whatsoever. Soon she completely lost the ability to speak. During the first Christmas when the crew of nurse's aides was too small, she developed excruciating bed sores which took months to heal.

But then an angel arrived on the scene in the form of a young black woman from Liberia whose name was Mary. She was a Christian and became a friend to Nonnie and to Mother. She took excellent care of Nonnie when she was on duty. I'm sure we owe the last months of Nonnie's life to her, but for some never-explained reason, Mary was suddenly moved from Nonnie's hall, and within two weeks, Nonnie was ill with a severe bladder infection.

At the same time, Grandad Arnold entered the hospital in Houston for his first bout with stomach cancer. Mother was torn, but she elected to go to be with him. She felt Nonnie had had so much of her time while Grandad had had so little. But by the time she returned three days later, Nonnie was in the hospital with a severe kidney infection and bowel impaction. Her heart failed, and she was gone within two days. She had lived eighty-seven years.

When a loved one has suffered so long, the first reaction is almost one of relief. But of course, the memories begin to flood in upon us, and we are surprised by knife thrusts of grief at unexpected times, for a long time. And for Mother and her siblings, there were the agonizing questions: What could they have done once she was in the nursing home to protect her from neglect? Could they have somehow kept her at home? When Mother and I talked about Nonnie's last years, I asked her what she would do differently if she had it to do over again.

"It helps to have all the knowledge about caring for elderly parents we can get," she said. "There are books, and even audio tapes, I discovered *after* it was all over that would have been helpful. I could have been more prepared than I was.

"But regardless of how well prepared we may be, I don't know anyone who has seen a beloved parent age and die who does not somehow struggle with guilt feelings at times. But you know, I think I've finally come to see that we can no more *completely* protect our parents from the hard things that come with growing old than they could protect *us* from the hardships of life they knew we would have to face in order to grow and mature. Sometimes getting out of this world is much harder than getting into it. But I'm very much looking forward to a reunion with her in heaven one of these days and talking it over with her. I have so many questions I'd like to ask her. This much I know—I grow more grateful with each passing day of my life that this life is not all there is."

I consider that our present sufferings are not worth comparing with the glory that will be revealed in us.

ROMANS 8:18, NIV

It's a Bird; It's a Plane; It's—Super Mom!

One of the nicest things about the arrival of my sister, Rachel's, newborn son Trevor was that it came very shortly after Nonnie left us, helping the hurt in us all.

Readers of our first book, *Worms in My Tea*, will not be surprised that Rachel majored in office management during college. In *Worms in My Tea*, I gave an example of what it was like for me, the right-brain creative type to have a sister who was clearly a left-brain organizer type. I wrote, "When we were children living at home, her belongings were so organized that I could not filch so much as one M&M from a mammoth Easter basket without being called to account for it." I don't know how she knew, but she always knew.

When Rachel moved back in with our parents after two years of being on her own, things generally went very well. She was determined to preserve her newly found independence and felt she was becoming more and more her own person. This was a great consolation until she realized just how independent the folks had become. While she had imagined them pining away after she, their last child, had left home, she was somewhat shaken to discover how well they had adjusted to their empty nest.

"Gee," she told me over the phone from Virginia, "it kind of hurt my feelings when I had to take Mom's face in my hands and say, 'Remember me? I'm Rachel—your daughter.'"

Eventually Rachel got a job in Virginia and settled there, getting her own apartment with a couple of great roommates. At this point, she felt she could relax. She was definitely her own person in her new surroundings, and she felt delightfully independent. Then she was invited to a wedding shower to which Mother was also invited. She chose her own gift, bought her own wrapping paper and ribbon, and got her own card, even though they both knew the bride and could have shared a gift. When she arrived at the party, she placed her gift in a huge pile of other gifts.

"There were probably a hundred gifts in that pile," she told me later on the phone, "and only two of them were wrapped in identical wrapping paper. Guess whose they were?" I could tell by the tone of her voice this was not what she had expected.

"Don't tell me. One was Mother's and the other belonged to my independent, one-of-a-kind little sister, perhaps?"

"Mom thought it was a hoot, of course," Rachel deadpanned.

"I have warned you about the omnipresent mother syndrome, haven't I? Mother even said that she hears Nonnie's advice whispering in her ear. It's comforting to know you're also experiencing this. Give it a few years and mark my words—you, I, and Mother will be virtual triplets."

In *Worms in My Tea,* I described the home births of my four children which took place during the "Mother Earth," "Back to Nature" era. To say I had been naive about the anesthetic effectiveness of proper breathing and good coaching during childbirth would be understatement at its grossest. I had been told that labor is merely hard work. I know hard work when I see it. Labor was *pain.* I wrote, "As memories of my totally natural Lamaze, LaBoyer, LaLudicrous births swept over me, all I could think was, *What was I thinking?*"

On the other hand, Rachel "went into labor after a full night's rest at about seven in the morning on her day off. Seven and a half hours later, she called me from the exquisitely beautiful and homelike birthing room at the hospital to tell me in graphic detail of the two painful contractions she had endured before calling for the epidural."

As you would expect of this couple and their new baby, they had spent long hours planning how they could manage to birth this baby and rear him without losing control or making mistakes. First and foremost in their plan was for the father to spend adequate time with his child, starting from the moment they took the baby home. Since I've been asked time and again how Rachel's serene and ordered life has survived the introduction of a child, I felt I should give an update.

The first thing that shattered my sister and her husband Gilley's composure was that Trevor cried. He cried, even when he couldn't possibly be hungry and when his diaper was toasty dry. Rachel, Gilley, and Mother spelled each other walking the floor at night for the first week or so, and the young couple's anguish knew no bounds. The new father could not find time to go to work what with all his new responsibilities at home, but when he called his boss to tell her so, there followed an interesting conversation.

"Ann," he told his boss, "I don't know when I'll be able to get back to work. The doctor has diagnosed our baby as having colic." The boss, being female and a mother of lengthy tenure, suppressed a smile.

"Gilley," she said, trying not to laugh, "the baby will be OK without you, but I may not. I'll see you tomorrow in the office, OK?"

Are you beginning to get the picture? In *Worms* I also wrote of baby Trevor, "I fully expect that my new nephew will . . . develop into a child prodigy at the piano, and as a teenager frequently ask, 'What else can I do to help you, Mother?'" Trevor is now age two-and-a-half, and after a recent telephone conversation with his mother, I have decided I may have been prematurely and overly envious.

"I've got to find a way to get organized," she said, and there was a ragged edge to her voice. "Working twenty hours a week shouldn't be that big a deal, should it? I feel like I'm losing control. Not long ago I had Trevor in the bathtub, and the phone rang. I debated about not answering it, but I was expecting an important call. I was close enough where I could hear him splashing and talking happily to himself, so I knew he was all right. Even so it took longer than I expected, and when I started back up the hall toward the bathroom, I could see water gently billowing onto the carpet.

"Just as I rounded the bend and threw on my brakes, Trevor was emptying the last toy bucket full of water out of the tub. THEN the doorbell rang. It was the designer-suited single gentleman from downstairs saying there was water leaking through the light fixture of his garage and onto his $30,000 Mercedes, and did I know anything about it. I only debated a few seconds before I told him what I knew about the guy who had done it, and promised him I'd see it didn't happen again.

"Fortunately we have a good friend who is an electrician, and we were able to prevail upon him to fix the fixture, but then last week I was rushing to get things together so I could get in to work. I had turned on the water faucet in the bathroom to let it warm up, and then I heard Trevor in the refrigerator in the kitchen. He's still in that 'take the lid off and pour stuff in the floor' stage, so I had to tend to him, and by the time I got the juice poured and his bib on and had him sitting at his feeding table, I remembered that I'd left the water running in my bathroom. (*My goodness*, I thought, *why didn't you just hand him the glass and get on with life!*)

"I took off down the hallway just in time to see the familiar water doing its familiar billowing toward the hall. I checked my watch to see how late I was going to be to work, and wondered if I could get out of the condo before Mr. Picky-About-His-Fancy-Car appeared at the door again. I told Scott that if he did, he was not to hesitate—tell him Trevor did it!"

Oh, this was delicious. Absolutely delicious, and, of course, when Mother and I met for lunch the next week, we had a great time laughing about Trevor's antics and his parents' efforts to manage them.

"I wonder if they ever think of that letter you wrote telling them what a great idea it is to have kids?" I asked.

"I don't know," she grinned, "but I may stay out of Virginia for a year or two. I may even need to ask forgiveness!"

Having finished lunch, she leaned back in her chair. I had the feeling there was something on her mind.

"Becky," she began, "I've been thinking a lot about forgiveness—how much it meant to me when your Granddaddy Jones let me know he regretted some of the bitter things that had passed between us. And I know I've made a lot of mistakes in raising *my* children. There are failures I'm aware of, but I expect there are failures in areas that were important to you that I don't even realize. Is there anything in particular that I need to ask your forgiveness for?"

"Well-l-l-l," I thought for a minute, and said the first thing that came to my mind. "I sort of wish you and Daddy had been more open about your arguments. Not that I wish you all had yelled at each other a lot or anything like that. But I'd like to have seen more conflict and clashing of opinions—like those earthy, emotional families from romantic Mediterranean countries do in the movies. Then I'd like to have observed the process of resolution.

It might have helped me not to have been so shocked when I had my first blowup with Scott. I think I grew up believing I'd never have a real fight with my husband." When I looked up from my salad, Mother had a very peculiar expression on her face.

"That's very interesting," she said, "because when I asked your sister the same question, she said she wished I could have controlled my anger a little more carefully. She probably had something in mind like those polite and respectful families from Asian countries from the movies. Isn't it interesting how differently siblings can see the same parent? I haven't yet asked David for forgiveness, but I plan to."

I could imagine already what David would say and had to laugh. "Let me save you the trouble, Mother. David would have preferred you to be more laid-back and easygoing—a 'no problem' type. Then we could all have lived like the happy natives in South Pacific movies."

Mother looked more confused than ever. Could even a super mom please every child? The more I thought about my own struggle to meet the individual needs of my four children, the more I empathized with my mother. I also felt a greater appreciation that she tried so hard and was trying even now to do the impossible.

"Hey," I said gently, "forget super mom. She's made out of plastic and paint, not flesh and blood."

"Thanks," she said, cupping her chin in her hand. "Actually, a little island vacation may sound pretty good by the time I finish this process. But you know what? You girls have surprised me. You didn't mention some failures on my part that I'm acutely aware of and wish I could undo. It never occurred to me that shielding you children from the disagreements your dad and I had might not be the best thing. I guess because there were so many storms swirling around my father in my childhood home, I was determined to shield my own children from that sort of thing.

"But of course, your dad and I *have* had some humdingers over the years, a few that were pretty serious. Does it help to know that?"

I nodded, somewhat relieved. Of course, mine and Scott's definition of a "humdinger" and Mother's and Daddy's definition might not exactly coincide. But at least I knew there had been a few chinks in my parents' relationship over the years, and it was reassuring.

Mother continued, "And I do apologize for ever trying to convey to you the image of perfection. Oh, Becky—life is real, and life is earnest. For everybody."

"You're right, I know," I answered seriously. Then in my brightest, most pleasant voice I asked, "You sure you and Daddy don't wanna try having a knockdown, drag-out, and throw spaghetti at each other—just to help loosen you up, tarnish that 'perfect' image a bit?"

Mother declined the invitation, but I still think it would have been a humdinger of an experience.

For all have sinned and fall short of the glory of God. . . .
There is now no condemnation
for those who are in Christ Jesus.

ROMANS 3:23; 8:1, NIV
❧

The Wind
Beneath Our Wings

You'll be pleased to know," Mother's voice came over the phone line from Houston, "that you are not the only members of the family who live their days among a wide variety of wild life. I've just gotten back from a stay with your Grandaddy Arnold, and I've decided even though he would never admit he likes animals, he's in the best possible place in the world for him, living with Buddy and Hazel. And I believe Aunt Hazel may have achieved her dream of a lifetime to be completely surrounded by dogs every waking hour. Their buying a house with a kennel attached is turning out beautifully for all concerned."

"How is Granddad?" I asked, uneasy about the answer to come.

"About as big as a bar of soap after a hard day's wash—mostly ears and nose now. Just a precious, walking bit of bones physically, but what a spirit! He still insists on getting up out of his easy chair and going to the kitchen for his own coffee most of the time. He's about decided the doctor was wrong about the stomach cancer."

"What does the doctor think?" I asked hopefully.

"He still thinks he was right," she said sadly.

It had been eighteen months since the diagnosis had been made. The doctor had told Uncle Buddy, my dad's brother, that Grandad had from two to six months to live, and it was Buddy's responsibility to tell him.

"Well," Grandad responded in his characteristic, matter-of-fact way, "if that's the way it is, that's the way it is. I'll get to see Margaret again. I hope I don't suffer, and I don't want a bunch of chemotherapy, and I don't want any operations."

"Whatever you say," Buddy replied.

But the months went by. Grandad had one spell in the early spring when his stomach blocked, and we all held our breaths and prayed. The blockage disappeared, and he went home from the hospital. At that point, his children and their spouses promised themselves that, unless he entered into unmanageable pain, he would live his life to the last at home, with the life of the kennel going on about him.

Alzheimer's had claimed Grandmother six years before, but even though he missed her with all his heart, he enjoyed life. He knew when his favorite shows came on television—political commentaries, quiz shows, and sports, sports, sports. He occupied the easy chair in the living room at Uncle Buddy's while the amazing adventures and the busy life of the kennel flowed around him in the blare of the TV, kept at top volume. While Grandad's mind was still sharp, his hearing was definitely not.

And when Aunt Ann and Uncle Don or Mother and Daddy came for a visit, they rigged up a bright light on the game table so Grandad could see the dominoes or cards, and he still whipped them all most of the time. It was about as good a life as one gets at his age, and he enjoyed it.

"I talk to myself every morning," he would tell us. "I say, 'Self, get out of that bed. Get your clothes on. You've got things to do and people to see.' And before you know it, I've made another day."

Through the huge picture window in the living room, he could sit in his easy chair, and when he wasn't watching one of his favorite TV shows, he could see an amazing variety of dogs prancing and barking in the pens—giant poodles looking ridiculous with their painted nails and bows in their hair, down to chihuahuas so tiny they were almost lost from sight among the leaves. He had dobermans and scotties and Lhasa apsos to observe, and occasionally a mastiff as big as a small pony.

Add to that the household pets—two Cairn terriers, an introverted spaniel, a tiny, prissy Pomeranian named Jaws, and one terribly nervous and shy white kitty. Throw in the kennel workers who were hardly less than family—Linda, Gwen, Becky, and others who came in and out all day for coffee, shared lunch with the family every day, who came to put Jaws and the others out for exercise—the constant ringing of the phone, the never-ending repairs and remodeling of the forty-year-old house and kennel—Grandad was sometimes irritated, but never bored.

After the diagnosis of Granddad's illness, Daddy's sister—my Aunt Ann—and her husband, my Uncle Don, came to Houston from Tucson often, parking their travel trailer under the big trees in front of the kennel. Mother and Daddy began to spend at least a weekend with him every month and a half or so. And Mother would occasionally go and spend several weekdays with her "buddy" as she now referred to him. She thrived on the goings on at the kennel and always came home with a story to tell.

"There's never a dull moment down there," she laughed over the phone. "Grandad and I were having our naps one day—he was stretched out in his recliner, and I was all snugged up on the couch with a pillow and an afghan. Kitty was lying along the top of the couch observing me. For some reason, that afternoon was wonderfully peaceful and quiet for a change, but then one of the kennel workers tiptoed in and opened the patio door to let the house dogs back in. They immediately spotted the cat and started barking. That scared the cat who landed in the middle of my stomach and then made it in one leap to the middle of Grandad's stomach. The dogs started to chase the cat, and the kennel worker started chasing the dogs.

"Grandad and I sat straight up looking wide-eyed at each other, and just then a young man we had never seen before opened the sliding glass doors. He walked in, said, 'Hi!' and disappeared into the back part of the house. Grandad and I looked at each other, shrugged our shoulders, flopped back in our respective places, and finished our naps."

"So what else do you do on these visits with your eighty-three-year-old father-in-law?" I asked.

"It's very pleasant, really. Buddy and Hazel are busy all the time, but they are wonderfully hospitable. The house is big and roomy, and they have a comfortable and private bedroom for guests, so I can catch up on reading. And I enjoy just sitting with Grandad while he dozes or watches television or listens to the big band sound of the forties on the radio. Usually he lets me give him a manicure, and sometimes he even lets me give him a pedicure."

I had seen one of the pedicures, with Mother sitting comfortably on the floor, gently lifting his swollen feet in and out of the pan of warm water, carefully trimming and clipping, then massaging with sweet smelling lotion. They talked only occasionally, smiling and relaxed in an easy rapport. It was obvious they both enjoyed the process. I smiled to myself, and Mother's voice on the other end of the wire brought me back to the present.

"He's very comfortable to be with, as you well know. We don't talk a lot, but occasionally he speaks of Margaret or the days when they traveled together and how much he enjoyed it. You know, we always imagined he would be a great talker if she would only hush, but the thing we never understood is that he didn't really want the center of the stage. We also never understood that, though their marriage seemed stormy and one-sided to us, he really loved her very much. Occasionally he will say, 'I still miss her.' But there has been a change in him in a major way. He has become so much more open about his love for his kids. Whenever Daddy and I talk with him on the phone now, he always signs off with, 'Love ya!' And this time when I left, he held my hand tight against his chest and said, 'I don't want you to go!'

"And it was *hard* to walk away. I'm pretty sure the next time I go, he will be bedfast. On the way back on the plane, I thought of how much in awe I was of him thirty-six years ago and how dear he has become to me. I've been doing a lot of thinking, of course. So much more is involved when we marry than we can possibly imagine. It really *is* a mystical union, and it's a union of more than just the bride and groom. So often the relationships we first have with our spouse's family are usually superficial and sometimes awkward. But with the passing of the years, they become a part of the warp and woof of our very lives—hopefully, for the better. Certainly your Grandaddy Arnold has become as much a father to me as my own father was. My life is so much richer for having known and loved him."

That was in January of 1991. Until then, Grandad had been saying he would like to live to be ninety—seven more years. But just before his eighty-second birthday came up in March, we got the news of his cancer. We decided to make it special and prayed he would still be feeling well enough to enjoy it. We were almost certain at the time we would not celebrate another with him. He surprised us, however.

Most of his friends had already gone home to be with the Lord, but Aunt Ann and Uncle Don came for the party, and all the kennel workers began to plan their remembrances. Mother invited all the Jones clan who lived in Houston. They all knew and greatly respected Lloyd Arnold. They would certainly be there for the party.

It happened that Aunt Hazel had a young friend who was also celebrating a birthday, and she invited Debbie Crow to come by for cake that Sunday afternoon. Debbie is a young black woman who had worked for Aunt Hazel as a secretary. She has a singing voice as big and as beautiful as a Colorado mountain, and she was also on the staff of her church. When Hazel told her over the phone we would be celebrating Grandad's birthday with a heavy heart, Debbie understood.

"Would you mind if I sang and ministered to your family while I'm there? I would really love to do that for you and your family and your dad."

So, when that beautiful, sunlit afternoon arrived, Debbie brought some accompaniment tapes, and after the cake, we all gathered in the den. Aunt Ann sat next to Grandad, holding his hand. Mother sat on the floor, leaning against his knee. None of us realized it at the time, but Daddy stood inside a doorway and filmed on video the golden moments that unfolded upon us as a magnificent gift.

Debbie's colossal voice filled the room in songs of praise for life, for the reality of a God who is Father as well as Creator, and for the very gift of family itself. And then, her voice softened, and she looked directly at Grandad and began to sing very softly:

"Did you ever know that you're my hero?
That you're everything I'd like to be?
I can fly higher than an eagle,
You are the wind beneath my wings."

In the words of that song, Debbie said to this good man all that was building and longing to be said in the hearts of his children and grandchildren. There were no dry eyes in the room, and on Grandad's wrinkled and tissue-thin cheeks sparkled the only tears I ever remember seeing there. I'll never forget the moment, and I'll always be grateful for having been there to see it. We all thought it would probably be our last family gathering with him on such a large scale.

A couple of years later, when Grandad began to be too weak to talk himself into getting out of bed and making one more day, visiting nurses came regularly to give medications. Ann and

Don parked their travel trailer under the trees and prepared to be there as long as they were needed. Mother and Daddy flew to Houston more frequently, rather than taking the six hours to drive. And on the night he left us, it was Mother's turn to be sitting with him.

He had had a restless, uncomfortable time, and she could not find a way to ease him. His eyes remained closed, and he drifted in and out of consciousness for several hours, often moaning softly and making a feeble effort to shift his position in the rented hospital bed. At about 3:00 A.M., she called Aunt Ann to come in from the trailer. Ann seemed to have an uncanny ability to know what her dad needed or to get him to tell her.

"Daddy," she called to him, hoping to penetrate to whatever state his mind had entered into. "Where do you hurt?"

"My feet!" he managed to say in a rapid, high-pitched but weak voice. "My feet!"

Mother and Aunt Ann were puzzled by this, but his feet were like ice, so they put a heating pad on them and sat on either side of the bed, rubbing them for a time. Soon, he seemed more comfortable and seemed to be sleeping. Ann had been up and down so many nights, she was very tired and went back to the trailer. Mother curled up in the lounge chair, and in the soft light of the lamp over her shoulder, drifted off to sleep.

At dawn, she was awakened by the sound of what she assumed was Grandad trying to clear his throat. He appeared to have congestion in his chest, and she made a mental note to discuss it with the doctor the next day. She stood by his bed, stroking his hand, but he seemed unaware.

How many more days, dear Lord, will he linger like this? she wondered. *Oh, please, take him home soon!* She went to the kitchen and made coffee and then brought her cup back to his bedroom where he lay in the hospital bed as she had left him . . . except he was breathing in the short and shallow breaths she had seen Nonnie enter into just hours before her death. She was shocked, because he had only been bedfast for two weeks. She walked to his bed and looked into the eyes that were now open and looking beyond her.

"You're going home *today*, aren't you?!" she said softly. "And, darlin', if you want to go right now, it'll be just fine." She turned to set her cup on the table beside his bed, and by the time she turned back again, he had taken two more breaths. There were no more.

When Mother called to tell me of Grandad's passing, I had been expecting her call. Blinking back my tears, I said, "It looks like your days as a member of the sandwich generation are over now."

"Yes," she said softly, "but I sure am going to miss the top slice of bread."

A gray head is a crown of glory;
it is found in the way of righteousness.
PROVERBS 16:31, NASB
❧

The Eagle Soars Home

El Shaddai, El Shaddai. . . . Age to age you're still the same."
Standing behind a screen among the funeral flowers, I sang
for the last time for my Grandad Arnold. He had been my last
living grandparent. This was the last goodbye my parents would
make to one of their parents. The night before, Mother had
written Grandad's eulogy, gleaning from each family member
the thing they most wanted to say about him and what he had
meant to each. My song ended, and the minister came to the
podium to read the bare statistics of his life—whom he married,
the number of children and grandchildren he had. Then my
mother took her place at the microphone, the eulogy in her
hand.

"I want to thank you on behalf of our family for coming here
today," her voice was steady, yet warm, "and I invite you to join
with us in some very personal remembrances of this good man.
His name was Lloyd Edward. His closest buddies often called
him L. E. or 'Speedy.' His wife, Margaret, called him 'Honey.'
His children called him 'Daddy,' even when he was eighty-five
and they were in their fifties. To his grandchildren, he was

'Grandad,' and those of us who were blessed to marry his children simply called him, 'Lloyd.'

"I remember as a nineteen-year-old bride adjusting to my new father-in-law and, being very much in awe of him, I experimented with titles ranging from 'Dad' to 'Mr. Arnold,' until one day he said with characteristic bluntness, 'Just call me Lloyd!'

"He was a spare man—never a spare pound on his body, and not many spare words on his lips. But what he said was worth waiting around to hear, more and more so as he grew older. As he advanced in age, he became more verbal about his love, more physical in his expressions of affection, more openly appreciative of kindnesses.

"As a young man, he played drums in a band, The Kansas City Night Hawks, and until three weeks before his death, he spent hours listening to the big band sound of the forties on his radio. He was a good dancer and enjoyed golf and bowling, the sort of sports that didn't require losing one's dignity. Margaret described him as dapper and sporty, and all the women liked to dance with him, often to her dismay.

"His son-in-law, Don, remembers him particularly as a good sport. Yesterday, we sat around the lunch table remembering Lloyd, and Don laughed as he remembered.

"'I'll never forget the day at Lake Gunnersville when we were trying to teach him to water ski. We dragged him all over that lake, but he *would* not give up, and he would *not* let go of that rope.'

"Lloyd's son, David, whom he always called 'Buddy,' added, 'He was a fierce competitor, without being overbearing or mean. He always tried to be the best he could be, whether it was a game of cards, dominoes, bowling, his work, or any other endeavor.'

"His son, George, wrote of him, 'He always encouraged the best in me. He set me free to fly and to find my own way, yet he was always there when I needed him. I'm going to miss so many things about him—watching the Astros on TV with him, games of forty-two and bridge, Sunday afternoon phone calls when we shared good news of all the family and signing off with his, "I love you, too!" I'll miss how he brightened when we came for a visit, and I'll miss just sitting in his presence with a cup of coffee. And I'll miss hugging him most of all.'

"For myself," Mother said, "I particularly remember that when any of us came to him for advice after we were adults, he would ask, 'Well, what do *you* think about it, George?' (or Ann? or Buddy?) And having given us the chance to think through and articulate what we really *did* think about the situation, he would say, 'I believe you're right. It'll work out.' If we needed a loan to make our dreams come true, all we had to do was ask. Then we would go on our way, stabilized and reassured and supported."

Mother's eyes met Daddy's, and they smiled. *Be careful, Mother. You've still got a lot left to say, I think.* She went on, her voice still strong.

"His first-born, Ann, remembers him in her childhood as a man who did not talk a great deal but who was kind when he did speak, and unfailingly 'there' for her. She remembers him coming in the door from work, making candy appear out of nowhere with a bit of sleight-of-hand. So deep is her love and loyalty to him that she resolved she would always be there for him. In his last weeks of life, she and Don moved their travel trailer adjacent to his home from their home in Tucson to be 'there' for him, however long he needed them. Ann assumed the primary responsibility to care for his most personal and private needs to the last hours of his life. Tenderly. Oh, so tenderly."

Mother's voice grew husky, and her eyes met Aunt Ann's, her sister-in-law of thirty-seven years. They had been close for a long time, but I sensed they were closer than they had ever been before after sharing that night vigil by Grandad's bed. Mother waited to regain her composure and then continued.

"Lloyd made his home the last ten years of his life with Buddy and Hazel, the first two years of that time along with his much loved Margaret. Buddy cooked his meals (always with an eye for good nutrition), ran his errands, and at the last, managed his finances, dealt with doctors, and handled all arrangements for his comfort and convenience to the day of his death.

"Buddy was caring for Lloyd at 3:00 A.M. on March 11, not knowing he was within the last hours of looking after his dad. Lloyd was uncomfortable and distressed, and Buddy was exhausted, feeling anguished frustration.

"'I love you, Daddy,' he said. 'I wish there was something I could do to help.' To his surprise, Lloyd heard him.

"'Go to bed,' was the response. How like him. It was a 'Lloydism,' the kind of characteristic remark that Hazel, especially, noticed and enjoyed about her father-in-law as she so graciously and freely shared her home with him. In remembering him, she had this to say:

"'I think of Lloyd as constant. In all the years I lived with him, he never spoke an unkind word about any person. He never looked on the negative side of anything. His memories of his life were positive and refreshing. When we needed a loan to start our kennel business, he was there for us.

"'About a week ago as his illness had gripped him so fiercely, I sat with him for a while one evening. It gave me an opportunity to say some things I very much wanted to say.

"'You've been a wonderful husband, a wonderful father, and a wonderful friend to many. You have a life to be very proud of.'

"'He answered simply, "Yes, I've had a good life."'"

Now Mother's eyes met Hazel's, her high school friend before becoming her sister-in-law. They smiled, and Mother then returned to her message:

"Had his life been an easy life? No. His mother died when he was a teenager in Houston, the third of ten children. The younger children were dispersed among relatives, and he was pretty much on his own. He once told Hazel in a rare, special moment of deep communication, 'I thought I'd never quit missing my mother.'

"Maybe that was why he was so careful to be sure he gave the love he felt his children and his grandchildren needed. I remember him bouncing our babies on his knee singing, 'Put your *e*, put your *i*, put your gimme a piece of pie, put your *e*, put your *a*, put your gimme a piece of cake.' And if that makes you think he had a wry, wonderful sense of humor, you would be right. All of us remember sayings from him like, 'I only like two kinds of pie—hot pie and cold pie.' And when he had one of us in a bind at the domino or bridge table, how he did love to gloat.

"'It's tough when it's like that,' he would say, 'and it's like that *now!*'

"Scott Freeman married our daughter and Lloyd's granddaughter, Becky. When he heard Lloyd had left us, he wept. 'I felt *liked* by him. We communicated well, sitting together in a room not talking.'

"Becky, who sang for her Grandad today, remembers a trip to the nursing home with him to see Margaret when Alzheimer's had cruelly disabled her mind and body. Becky said, 'As he brushed away the tears, I saw a living example of what wedding vows mean—faithfulness until death parts us, in a world where those vows don't mean a whole lot anymore.'

"Our son, David, remembers a visit to Grandad when he was ten years old. 'He woke me at 4:30 A.M. to go fishing. The toast was already made, and he poured me a cup of coffee as if I were his best fishing buddy. When Grandad couldn't see to drive on the freeways anymore, he gave me his car.'

"Ann and Don's son, another Scott, who is not here today, flew in from Colorado three weeks ago, choosing to spend a weekend with his grandad while he was living. He sat for hours in the room with him, his long legs stretched out before him, enjoying that same comfortable communication that didn't require talking.

"Scott's brother, Jim, remembers his generosity also. 'In '81 when I was offered a good job in California, Valerie and I didn't have the money to make the move. Grandad loaned me the money, and without that loan, I might not have the good life I have today.'

"Valerie remembers Lloyd's unusual habit of counting things—bricks in a wall, stairs in a staircase, cards in a deck, spots on dominoes. He played his last game of forty-two with us in January. And yes, he won as usual.

"Lloyd took his family through the years of the depression, never actually losing his job at Lone Star Cement Corporation. He never worked for another company, and with less than a high school education, he made his way up the ranks to office and accounting manager where his aptitude with numbers and his penchant for order and logic made him a natural. His innate, understated kindness and calling forth of the best in people made him a loved and respected boss and coworker. When he retired, Lone Star called him back as a consultant to travel the United States with Margaret for another ten years. They called themselves 'The Lone Star Road Runners,' and they had a ball.

"How did this man come to such a successful conclusion, so loved that his three children and their spouses were determined to allow him to play out his hand in his own home, in his own bed, with his own loved ones caring for him?

"He was not a philosopher, but he had a philosophy. He was not a man who was adrift. He *really* believed in the law of love. If he had a blind spot, it was in his loving; he looked beyond the faults and woundings of those he loved.

"I well remember a day in our home when we were involved in a deep theological discussion with Margaret. He walked through the room and said quite matter-of-factly, 'It's simple. Jesus died for my sins. I accept that.' Then he walked away, leaving us all blinking after him.

"He believed firmly that he had a guardian angel whose personal business it was to look after him, and he expected things to work out well. Put more spiritually, he believed Romans 8:28, 'All things work together for good to those who love God and who are the called according to His purposes.'

"Our daughter, Rachel, who could not be here today, wrote to her grandad on February 13 of this year, three weeks before he died:

Grandad, our aging, failing bodies are testimony to the fact that we live in a temporary environment here on earth. Please don't get so focused on your failing body right now and think your *body* is what makes up *you*. *You* are a kind, giving, intelligent *spiritual* man.

Just as God somehow puts a spirit into a newborn baby's body, He will somehow put your beautiful spirit into a new body. I imagine that you will have a strong young body very soon that will hold Grandmother close and twirl her around a big, celestial dance floor.

Mother smiled with the people gathered there, and continued.

And *I* expect there will be a celestial band playing their song, 'I'm in love with you, Honey. Say you love me, too, Honey. No one else will do, Honey. Seems funny, but it's true.'

"Being the orderly person that he was, he celebrated his eighty-sixth birthday on Wednesday, March 10, and then took his leave of us the following morning. Being the positive person that he was, he left us in the spring of the year when everything that surrounds us speaks of resurrected life. Being the considerate person that he was, always trying to make things easy for us, he left on a Thursday so that we could all more conveniently celebrate his homegoing on a Saturday afternoon, giving us plenty of time to get back home and to work by Monday morning.

"Several weeks ago he told Ann, 'You kids need to get on with your lives.' I'm sure that's what he would say to us today, and so we shall take his advice and do just that. And, family, can't you almost hear him rattling his car keys and saying, 'Let's go! I'm a million dollars waitin' on a dime!'"

Mother's face was radiant as she returned to her seat.

Let not your heart be troubled: ye believe in God,
believe also in me.
In my Father's house are many mansions:
if it were not so, I would have told you.
I go to prepare a place for you.

JOHN 14:1–2, KJV
ॐ

A Nest of My Own

Our Very Own Bird's Nest on the Ground

My mother grew up dirt poor in an old house with dusty wood floors, a house where no one ever knew which room or bed or brother or sister they'd end up sleeping with at the end of a long day. Imagine her delight when she married my father who took her away from all that to a brand new home in the suburbs complete with built-in appliances, a fireplace, plush carpet, two bathrooms, and separate bedrooms for each child.

Imagine then her shock when my husband and I moved our four children to the country into a small cabin with dusty wood floors, a house where no one ever knew which room or bed or or brother or sister they'd end up sleeping with at the end of a long day.

Clearly, there is a vast difference between the housing preferences and lifestyles my mother and I have chosen, whether out of choice or necessity, I'm not always altogether sure. At least my little family is surrounded by leafy timber and sparkling water, but anyway you look at it, we seem to have created our own private demographical niche. Scott and I like to think of ourselves as baby boomers in the boonies.

From the time I was a young girl I dreamed of living in a cottage, complete with picket fence, nestled somewhere in Goldilock's forest. I've since learned there is more to living near the edge of the forest than an adorable family of talking bears and bowls of steaming hot porridge. And some of the intruders who have shown up in our backyard have very little in common with innocent little girls wearing satin ribbons in their boing-yoing curls.

Neither did I imagine that the cottages I had loved in childhood fairy tales did not come equipped with dishwashers, disposals, and central heat and air. The picket fence didn't materialize, either. I soon learned that picket fences do not good neighbors make in this laid-back, lakeshore community. Some days, actually, I have felt I could use a fence something on the order of the ones they used in Jurassic Park—like on the day Gabe came running into the house, his eyes bugging out.

"Mom!" he shouted, "there are cows in our backyard! And they've got humongous things sticking out of their heads."

Right. Of course. Children do have such creative imaginations, don't they? However, at Gabe's insistence, I decided to humor him by following his skipping, pointing form outside to see whatever he had imagined. And there they were—a nice little herd of Texas longhorns, grazing happily in my backyard. Gabe and I stood in the doorway and watched them for about ten minutes, and eventually they lumbered off into the woods, never to be seen again.

The longhorn cattle were probably the largest animals we have entertained (so far), but there have been any number of other interesting visitors from the nearby enchanted woods. For several weeks, a furry family of baby possums occupied our laundry room. Among their other activities, they enjoyed a curious game of peek-a-boo at my husband as he ironed his shirt in the mornings. (I'd say that *I* was ironing his shirt, but then this story really *would* be a fairy tale.) Like so many species, possums are actually quite cute until they get to be teenagers.

During their rocky adolescence they sprout needle sharp teeth, stay out all night having wild parties, and deposit revolting possum pellets in clothes hampers full of freshly folded laundry. And if you think a cat has nine lives—wait until you try to say *adiós* to a possum. Take our advice and forget it. They are immortal.

Because of the wildlife refuge atmosphere of our home, we have a major concern when city dwellers come to stay with us overnight. Take the time my father came out for a visit while Mother was away visiting Nonnie. This was back when our house was basically a large one-room cabin, Abe Lincoln style. Daddy slept on the fold-out couch maybe fifteen feet away from where Scott and I snoozed in our double bed, which barely fit into the opposite corner of the room.

Perhaps I should pause here to explain that the simple act of folding out the couch in front of an audience causes beads of perspiration to appear on Scott's forehead. You see, we never know what may be lurking under the cushions and between the springs of our couches, particularly if they haven't been unfolded in a while. We and our guests have been treated to several hair-raising surprises over the years. Among the items most fondly remembered are the peanut butter sandwich resembling petrified wood, a small and squeaking mouse, the skeleton of a red-eared turtle, some skimpy blue lingerie (Scott's brother found that little item), and an impressive assortment of fuzz and long-deceased insects.

After Daddy observed all this preparation of his bed for the night, he suggested that the next time we opened the couch, we should have a baseball bat and a can of insect spray handy. Had we known what lay ahead in the wee hours of the morning, we could have said, "And you ain't seen *nothin'* yet!"

At about 2:00 A.M., Gabe's pet anole (a green chameleon-type lizard) decided to explore my forehead. I was taken by surprise, to put it mildly. I bolted upright and screamed, waking Scott and Daddy and all creatures great and small as far away as the other side of the lake. Once Scott got through to me, and I realized the intruder was harmless, I fell back onto my pillow with a thud and into the sound stages of deep and dreamlike sleep. Daddy, however, stayed wide-awake until morning.

So. Why are we here in a cabin in the woods instead of living in a condo overlooking a golf course? I'll be honest. It is partly preference, and partly financial necessity. We wanted to raise our children in the country, preferably on a lake, and this cabin was what we could afford. As God provides us with a little money here and there, we've been able to add on, inch by inch. And we never looked back once we made the decision to live here. Even when the sewer backed up and the toothed critters threw nocturnal parties, Scott and I declared this to be "Home, Sweet Home." This piece of ground is where our roots are sinking. It's where I want to watch my grandchildren fish and swim and teach them to say, "Great Blue Heron."

Like the pioneer man and woman of *Little House* days, Scott and I take mutual pride in building a homestead, plank by plank. Of course, I'm speaking figuratively about my actual involvement in the homebuilding projects. Most of my heavy efforts involve asking, "Do y'all want some iced tea?"

Scott's family, especially his dad, have put in many hours of "barn raisin'" on our behalf. My folks have contributed elbow grease, paint, curtains, and decorative touches. Both sets of parents have made generous financial donations to "the cause" on special occasions—pure gifts of love. Even Zach and Zeke are hammering on the construction of what will someday be their upstairs loft. It's been quite the extended family affair.

Still, my mother sometimes worries, as all mothers do, about my happiness and contentment. Not long ago at a book signing, we had a *few* minutes to chat between the *throngs* of customers standing before us. We had just time to cover the entire theological foundations of American history and how many angels could fit on the head of a pin, and then went on to the more mundane events of life—like longhorn cattle in the flower garden and possum fangs in the laundry room. Finally she asked me a question I think may have been on her mind for some time. "Becky, do you feel like you've had a hard life?"

I knew she was comparing my life to hers when she had been my age. We had talked about this in a general way before that, as my generation settles into adulthood, our lives are very different from the lives of her generation at the same stage in life.

"I think," Mother had often said, "that my generation was privileged to live for a few brief years in a golden blip in time. A college degree in the fifties almost automatically meant a stable job in a stable company, a nice home, a new car. It wasn't that hard to have 'the good life.'"

On the other hand, my generation, the Baby Boomers, have not found the steps to the good life as easy to climb. College degrees in some fields are often a dime a dozen. As a result we tend to overextend our credit cards to live up to the image of "settled adults" that we remember from childhood. But things are not the same for us. They simply *are not*.

My friend and insightful author, Paula Rinehart, has written a book that helped Mother and me both understand the dreams and disappointments faced by my generation. It is aptly titled, *The Cleaver's Don't Live Here Anymore* (Chicago: Moody Press, 1993). In comparing Mother's postwar generation to my crowded boom generation, Paula writes, "The fine irony is that our experience is practically the reverse of our parents'. The hardest years of their lives, were, for the most part, their early years—the proving ground from which they moved on to better things" (p. 47).

For much of my generation, the reality is that we have already lived out the most prosperous portion of our lives—and it happened to have taken place in our childhood. The adult portion of our lives may prove to be the most economically difficult for many of us. And because we had such high expectations of success, our generation has had to deal with a few unpleasant realities—like we can't have everything we want when we want it without getting in so deep over our heads that we will possibly never see daylight again.

Mother's generation had been thoroughly warned about debt by frugal parents who drummed into them the importance of living within one's income. Once television commercials and easy credit permeated the very air we breathe, many of them often forgot the ancient wisdom and many of their children were never told.

Ah, well. So how did I answer Mother's question, "Do you feel like you've had a hard life?" Actually, the answer came easily.

"No, I really don't." I paused and reflected on my reasoning. "Sure, there have been struggles and disappointments and even jealousy at times over what you and Daddy were able to have—and on one income. But, somewhere fairly early along our way, I gave up those comparisons.

"Instead, I found myself reading stories of people in India and other poverty-stricken countries. I read the true story of Corrie Ten Boom's life in a Nazi concentration camp. Alongside these people's life experiences, I felt spoiled and rich at the mere thought of having a roof over my head, food to eat, and a family that loved me."

Mother was smiling, and her eyes reflected something wonderful to me. Was it respect? Maybe even, pride in what I was saying?

"For me," I went on, "it boils down to this. I can compare myself to *The Lifestyles of the Rich and Famous* or the starving in Africa. One encourages discontent; the other, immense gratitude. I'd lots rather spend my days with a thankful heart."

It was a good conversation to have with my mother. I think she felt better about our choice, and it gave me an opportunity to put into words what I had been feeling and thinking without realizing it. *Wow*, I thought, *I now have a philosophy of life of my very own, and I think my mother approves!* The unseen branch under my imaginary nest felt somehow stronger and sturdier.

Mother had asked me an interesting question, and since I've started writing, other people sometimes ask me questions, too. One I hear fairly often is, "How do you cope with the irritations in your life—how can you laugh at what other people see as humiliating disasters?"

I often answer with the eloquence of a well-seasoned philosopher, "I have really low standards."

Seriously, I can assure my mother that I am truly happy and content. In most ways, I honestly wouldn't trade my lifestyle for the one my mother chose and was able to afford at my age—even with the lizards, possums, and longhorns that occasionally visit our nest in this "branch" of the woods.

Finally, brothers, whatever is . . .
excellent or praiseworthy—think about such things . . .
for I have learned to be content whatever the circum-
stances. I know what it is to be in need, and I know what it
is to have plenty. I have learned the secret of being content
in any and every situation.

PHILIPPIANS 4:8, 11–12A, NIV

Birds of a Feather
Still Flock Together

We had wondered if the Jones family would be the same after Nonnie was gone. I soon found that attending a Jones Family Reunion is still an Amazing Experience. Each time we gather with my mother's side of the family and everybody reports on what they've been up to, I always feel like asking, "Do other families do these kinds of things?" And a voice from deep inside whispers, "I don't *think* so!"

As one might expect, this is a crowded, noisy, lots-of-hugging, whoop-it-up, chocolate-covered affair. Aunt Etta flies in from Lubbock with no less than twelve chocolate cream pies. A lesser woman would have concluded it couldn't be done, but not my Aunt Etta. She bakes the twelve pie shells and stacks them one on top of the other in a hat box which she carries onto the plane, the hat box swinging from one arm. Of course all this is accomplished with style, charm, and excellent posture. The gallon of chocolate cream filling is divided into two plastic containers and stowed in a shopping bag which she swings from the other arm. Whipped topping is purchased on arrival in Houston, and the orgy is on. I've always wondered what the other passengers on her plane might look like in the event of severe turbulence or a rough landing. All I know is that my Aunt Etta would be the picture of poise and grace even with a face full of pie filling.

Aunt Etta also stows away in her luggage a dreamy concoction called Lemon Poppyseed Bread, which Uncle Genie insists on referring to as "Lemon Puppy's Knuckle Bread." This is the same uncle who entertained us by remembering the night some years back when he and his wife, my Aunt Deon, put their kids to bed and decided to make a dress form for her out of plaster of paris. She would, however, have to be the model while the plaster molded and then hardened. The two problems they had neglected to plan for were (1) how they were going to get the thing off when it dried and (2) plaster of paris gets hot when it dries. Uncle Genie finished the story for us.

"You should have seen how fast I clawed through my tool box looking for snippers big enough to cut through plaster of paris!"

Aunt Deon is a quiet, unassuming lady who probably should have been an engineer. Uncle Genie is not quiet and is altogether assuming—assuming he can accomplish any project Aunt Deon might dream up. She takes delight in dreaming up the projects, he takes delight in attempting things that angels would not dare.

There was the day he came up with the ingenious notion to unstop a sewer line with an air compressor while Aunt Deon watched at the other end of the line. The plan was that she would tell him when the sludge loosened up and began to flow out of the pipe. Anyway, that was the plan. Actually, it worked quite well—too well, in fact.

When Aunt Deon bent down to check on the progress, the air-powered sludge came roaring out to greet her, right in the face. While the rest of us whooped over that one, Aunt Deon emitted her gentle, little "Hoo, hoo, hoo" chuckle. Through it all, Uncle Genie managed to keep a straight face, insisting it was a good idea that should have worked.

"It was somewhat like the time Deon had made a new pillow case for an old feather pillow," he went on. "We had bought a new vacuum cleaner, and the salesman had assured us it could just about clean the house all by itself, not to mention the garage. It seemed logical to Deon that we ought to be able to blow the feathers directly from the old pillow case into the new one, using the new vacuum cleaner."

Already we had the picture, but he finished the story as expected. "Twenty years later when we remodeled our kitchen we were still finding feathers in the rafters and behind sheet rock." He shook his head sadly. "Shoulda worked."

So much for the latest from the Gene Jones family.

Uncle J. R. was just back from Pennsylvania where he had gone to appear as a contestant on Bill Cosby's quiz show, "You Bet Your Life." Cosby chose him to match wits with other contestants on the show because Uncle J. R. is a bit unusual. At age fifty-seven, he was the Texas State Arm Wrestling Champion, regularly defeating surprised young men in their twenties.

By this time, our colossal dinner had settled, and we headed for the kitchen to load dessert plates with another round of Aunt Etta's chocolate pie. We regathered at the table, and my cousin Jamie—Uncle J. R.'s daughter—joined us.

Now, I feel I must prepare you for Jamie. If any statement in this book stretches the reader's capacity to believe, it will be this one: I am not the only person in the world who can make chaos out of virtually any situation without the slightest intention to do so. I have a counterpart in my cousin Jamie.

When people meet Jamie for the first time, they expect her to be, well, . . . "together." When she began to hold forth at the reunion with her latest escapades, she looked more like a gorgeous TV personality about to present a commentary on world events. Her enormous blue eyes danced with life in a beautifully tanned face. Frame the cherry red mouth with dimples and the tanned face with cascading golden blonde hair, and you begin to get the picture. She sat quite relaxed with her long, tapered hands folded over crossed knees, reminiscing about her days as an aide in a California nursing home. How did this knockout blonde happen to be working as a nurse's aide in a place where the young usually don't hang out? Let's put it this way. In a Miss America pageant, Jamie would have been chosen Miss Compassionate. On that warm, sunny afternoon in Houston she told us one story after another of her adventures in the nursing home.

"The hardest part about my job," she began, "was never having enough help. I had twelve patients to bathe and care for in an eight-hour period, so I never felt I was doing a really good job for any of them. They were precious to me, though, and I loved them, bless their hearts.

"One of my favorite patients was an ex-Aggie football player named Spike. He couldn't see, and he couldn't walk or talk, but he *loved* for any of the staff to ball up a pillow and throw it into his stomach like a football. The minute he felt that pillow land in his mid-section, he'd grab it and hold it in the air like a football player who had just snagged an impossible pass. Then he'd duck his head, tuck the pillow under one arm, and bounce up and down in his wheel chair, mentally heading for the goal line. You could almost hear the roar of the crowd. I thought Spike was a ton of fun, and we played lots of football together. But I never heard Spike say a word.

"After I had been there a couple of weeks, the director sent me to Spike's room with his usual oatmeal. 'Test it to make sure it's not too hot,' she warned. So I went to Spike's room and found him sitting in his wheel chair. If I hadn't had a breakfast tray in my hands I would have thrown him a pass to let him know I was there.

"Hi, Spike," I greeted cheerily, "how you doin'?" He grinned his toothless grin, but made nary a sound. He had dropped his lap cover, so I found that for him and covered his feet and legs. Then I had to get myself a chair and by the time I was situated, I had forgotten all about the director's warning. Finally I scooped up a big bite of oatmeal and dumped it into Spike's eager mouth. I soon learned that Spike could speak after all. He yelled at the top of his lungs, '#@&*%! *That's hot!*'"

Listening to her story, we all had a good laugh and begged for more, so Jamie went on to tell us about her experience with the all new electric beds in one of the nursing homes where she worked as a temporary.

"At all of the other places I had worked, we had to crank those beds to elevate them, and since I'm tall, I was really tickled to discover that I could not only raise or lower the head of the bed, but the whole bed would rise slowly when I punched the right button. So one evening I went in to get Mr. Shropshire ready for bed by helping him brush his teeth. Before I went in to the bathroom to get his toothbrush I punched the button to elevate his bed. When I got to the bathroom, I noticed someone had put one of his undershirts in the sink to soak, so I decided to rinse it out and hang it up to dry. Just about the time I got to the wringing-out part of my chore, I heard a loud crash and a bang and then a scraping sound. I dropped the T-shirt and ran back into the room.

"You couldn't believe how high those electric beds would go! Mr. Shropshire was now even with my chest (remember, I'm tall), but that was not my biggest problem. Evidently the rail of the bed had caught the night stand on the way up, and it was wedged between the bed and the wall. While I stood there, the radio slid off the stand and onto the patient's bed, grazing him lightly on the side of the head before coming to a stop just under his chin. I didn't know whether to laugh or cry, but once I apologized, Mr. Shropshire didn't seem particularly upset."

We loved that story, too, and figured Mr. Shropshire probably thought he had been carried to the sky by the beautiful angel hovering over him.

"Here's one I almost forgot," she giggled. "Now this happened while I was still in training, so it's understandable, OK?

"There was a Mr. Williams who needed help putting his false teeth in. He didn't particularly like to wear them and would have been more than happy just to gum it, but we always tried to make sure he had them in his mouth for meals. This particular morning, I was in a hurry, so I whipped those dentures out and approached his wheel chair.

"Come on, Mr. Williams, it's time for breakfast. I'm going to put your teeth in. Open wide." He looked at me like he had no idea what I was talking about, so I opened his mouth for him, popped 'em in, and wheeled him into the dining room. I gave all the patients a tray and then observed them to make sure no one needed assistance.

"Just then I noticed Mr. Williams having trouble chewing his strawberries. This was odd, because Mr. Williams loved to eat, especially strawberries, and I had never noticed him having trouble chewing anything before. I walked over to investigate, and when he looked up at me, I was confronted by the strangest set of dentures I had ever seen in my life. The top teeth were quite small, and the bottom teeth much bigger, giving Mr. Williams the appearance of a Pekinese dog. When it hit me that I had put the bottom plate on top and the top plate on the bottom, I started to laugh. I couldn't help it. I laughed 'til the tears ran down my face. I couldn't stop laughing and had to get someone else to put Mr. William's teeth in right so he could eat his breakfast."

Now I ask you. *Do* other families do these kinds of things? I still don't think so!

While I and several of my cousins sat among the older generation of Joneses telling our stories with the best of them, I remembered those reunions I had attended out in West Texas as a child. The kids had played games in the living room floor while the grown-ups had sat around the table after the meal telling tall and hilarious tales. Now, we were grown-ups, too. By Jove, we even got a little respect now and then!

When the party ended and good-byes could no longer be postponed, I watched each of my uncles individually take both Mother and Aunt Etta tenderly into their arms and kiss them, murmuring things like, "Bye bye, sweetie," and "See you next time, sugar."

Aunts and cousins hugged and laughed like a gaggle of geese, each trying to outdo the other with their parting shots. Aunt Martha hugged me and warned, "Watch those kiddos, Becky. Don't let 'em sneak up on you and throw you in the lake, now!"

I settled into the car next to Mother, tired, happy and ready to be home again. I had survived another Jones family reunion where we had laughed a lot, loved a lot, and eaten way too much once again. But still, it was a wonderful feeling. The "birds" in our family tree had rearranged themselves a bit, but the roots were still deep and strong, the trunk solid. And down among the lower branches, I thought I could almost make out the silhouette of a new nest. Wait—was that "Mr. and Mrs. Scott Freeman and Brood" written on the mailbox?

God sets the lonely in families.

PSALM 68:6

Long Live the Lovebirds!

B ecky," Scott said with compassion in his voice, "it's late. Peb may not appreciate a phone call at this time of night, especially for free medical advice."

I thought about that. Peb cherished and guarded his time "off the clock" and made it known that when he was not on duty—he was *not on duty*. We first met young Dr. Peb Smith and his tiny, very sweet wife, Lori, years ago when we moved to the lake. They owned a cabin up the road from ours, so I quickly got acquainted with Lori. After a couple of years of knowing them, Gabe summed up Lori in one simple statement:

"Mom, the nicest people in the world are God and Lori." There are a few theological problems with that statement, but basically I must concur.

The first time we met Peb, we were sure he didn't like us at all. He was quiet and reserved, eyeing us suspiciously, standing with arms crossed over his chest as he tugged at his beard. While Lori fussed over us with her friendly chatter, Peb uttered barely a word. Over time, we've learned that though Peb is quiet by nature, he has a big heart once he warms up to you. As a matter of fact, I have a hard time imagining him in a white coat and stethoscope since we only see him at church dressed in a suit or running around in shorts and a T-shirt at the lake.

I soon noticed how tender Peb was with his children and the way he took delight in animals of any sort. He once showed up at my back door grinning from ear to ear, carrying a bullfrog as big as a small dog. He had driven over with his new pet just to see my reaction. I thought at the time it was kind of God to give this man three little boys so he would have an excuse to play with large bullfrogs.

He often asks Gabe to join him and his youngest son, Kendy, to go out in his boat to fish for crappie. After one such excursion, Gabe began to formulate his opinion of Dr. Smith.

"Peb is really growing up," he told me. "He's talking a whole lot more now." Before long, Gabriel was so impressed with the man that he said, "I want to be a doctor when I grow up, just like Peb."

"Why, honey?" I probed, waiting to hear a speech from my child prodigy about benefiting humanity and so forth.

"Because," he replied as if I should already know, "a doctor gets to find turtles and go fishing for *his* job." Neither Peb nor I had the heart to tell Gabe anything different. Later perhaps.

Over the years, Scott and Peb often took the boys camping, and Lori and I enjoyed regular lunch dates filled with girl talk. But right now, I needed to hear the sound of Peb's steady, reserved voice giving out medical advice, even if it might irritate him that I was calling after hours. I knew Peb never pulled any punches just to spare someone's feelings. I could get the unadulterated truth from him. Soon I had the good doctor on the other end of the line.

"Peb, this is Becky," I said without formalities. "I can't get to sleep because there's a huge lump in my throat. No, it's not my tonsils; it's my mother. . . . No, my mother is not in my throat. . . . Oh, Peb, she's having some kind of test tomorrow— an arteriogram I think they called it. It sounds awful—I think they're going to put a scrub brush tied to a long rope through the main artery in her leg. I'm afraid it might be dangerous, I love her so much, and I just can't lose her now, and. . . . What? . . . No big deal, you say? . . . Routine? . . . Peb? . . . Did I ever tell you I think you're the best turtle-hunting, frog-catching, fisherman doctor in Hunt County? Thank you, thank you, thank you!"

After the series of illness and deaths of my grandparents, I guess I had gotten a little paranoid. With Peb's reassurance, I enjoyed a good night's sleep, then the next morning made the hour and a half drive to the hospital where Mother lay, already peacefully recuperating from her test (which came out well, by the way, and so did the scrub brush). She could even spell "cantaloupe," and I'm not so sure she could *before* the test.

She looked so pretty, so sweet, so fragile lying in the hospital bed. Even in this sterile environment, she seemed completely at ease, and she and Daddy were already gently ribbing each other. Daddy looked at me with love and relief in his moist eyes.

"Isn't your mother something?" he asked softly.

I met him with eyes full of the same love and relief and answered easily. "She sure is, Daddy."

There's something about seeing your loved one in a hospital setting that pulls out all the love stored in your heart for them. What we were really thinking, what was too painful to voice, was *Oh, God, what would either of us do without her?* Even while I type this, the lump comes back in my throat, and the tears spill down my cheeks. And I wonder how grown children survive the loss of parents they love, and I pray fervently that the Lord will rapture me to heaven before I have to deal with that little passage in life.

But I, the eternal optimist, am determined to see that my parents can beat this aging thing. Why *couldn't* they be the first couple in the history of the world to grow young? I've been collecting a file for some time now on people who live loooooong happy lives. Once I get all the data collected, I'm going to force—yes, at gunpoint, if necessary—my mother and father to follow every step to keep themselves healthy and brilliant until they are at least one hundred years old. I've already got quite a collection.

First, I've got a little array of encouraging statistics. According to an old issue (dated March 1986) of *Home Life* magazine that I found stuck under a drawer, the life expectancy in 1900 was 46 for men and 48 for women. According to the article, the life expectancy has now grown to age 70 for males and 79 for females. Since my research is nine years old at this writing and the yellowed article smells like old cedar, I'm sure that the average life expectancy is up by at least twenty more years by now. Listen to this: "Researchers speak of persons living to 110 years of age in the future, with the average to be in the upper 80s." From this evidence, I draw the conclusion that my mother and father are mere babes—barely old enough to be out past 10:00 P.M. at night. (This is fun. I love writing serious research. I wonder if Ted Koppel needs an assistant?)

More good news: according to another of my respected medical journals, *Woman's Day Magazine* (February 1994), older persons who are physically active measure "ten to fifteen years younger than their chronological age." Since I do not exercise much, and my parents exercise everyday like faithful hamsters on a treadmill, I've figured out that in actual "fitness years" my parents are about three years younger than I am.

In the *Greenville Herald Banner*, which, of course, is second only to the *Wall Street Journal*, I found a fascinating story distributed by the Associated Press in November of 1993. It's based on three million dollars worth of research into centenarians who never lose their quality of life. For the three million bucks, we learn the following: "Optimism, the ability to cope, and religion or some similar guiding philosophy link the healthiest, most independent centenarians." I think my parents rate high in all three categories, and I'm feeling more optimistic even as I write.

This article goes on to say that an "advanced education and an imaginative, opinionated personality help, too. . . ." Whew! If being opinionated helps, look out Methuselah! Mother and Daddy both read thick books on history and philosophy like a couple of college nerds. I'd give my folks a ten in all three of these categories. They could easily be voted "Most Likely to Live to Be 100 and Love Every Minute of It."

The article further listed a collection of characters filed under "Old Geezer Heroes." For example, Phillip Robinson, one hundred, of Georgia, remembers watching troops go off to the Spanish American War when he was a boy of five. He advises, "Moderation in all things. And have good friends, do what you enjoy if you can and be interested in things."

Another local hero is Dr. Michael DeBakey of Houston, Texas. According to the *Dallas Morning News*, September 5, 1993, Dr. DeBakey, eighty-five-year-old world famous heart surgeon and medical statesman, "gets to his office by 7:00 A.M. daily and spends many mornings in complicated cardiovascular surgery. He still sees patients from around the world, teaches young doctors, gives advice to other specialists, makes rounds at the hospital and does research. It's often 8:00 P.M. before he wheels his racy Volkswagen sports car out of the garage and goes home to his wife, Katrin, thirty-five years younger than he. Even at home, he often reads and writes into the night."

I must ask Mother if she's ever considered going to medical school to become a heart surgeon. I think it's important for her to begin to think about what she wants to be when she grows up.

And what about Paul Reese, who at age seventy-three ran a marathon *a day* (26 miles) for four months, eventually running 3,192 miles across the United States? But I'm thinking that it might be hard to convince Mother to squeeze a quick marathon into her daily routine.

However, I think I may have found just the sport for those who want to age with grace, dignity, and "whee!" At age 100,

Mr. S. L Potter (he says the S. L. stands for "Stupid and Lazy") was recently congratulated by *Today's* Willard Scott for climbing, and then bungee jumping from, the highest tower (210 ft.) in North America. I'm thinking of offering Mother a deal—she lives to be a centenarian, and I'll take her bungee jumping.

But my favorite hero among the gracefully aging is Billy Graham. Right now I'm looking in my files at a magnificent portrait of him from *Time* magazine's excellent cover story, "A Christian in Winter" (November 1993).

If I were to do a word association at this minute, based on what I read of Graham, I would have to borrow a phrase from the title of one of my favorite books written by my friend, Bob Briner. The title of the book and my title for Billy Graham, precious friend of God, would be almost the same: *Roaring Lamb*. Mr. Graham has been a lion who roars, an outspoken evangelist who's proven to be above reproach and well-respected in the secular world, too. He has befriended presidents and peasants.

Interestingly, Graham said, "I've always thought my life would be a short one." Surprise! God's plans are not always according to our intuitions. I love the way Graham looks at life now, even though he's been stricken with Parkinson's disease.

"It doesn't make me feel any different, turning seventy-five, than when I turned forty-five," he muses. "But when I see pictures of my nineteen grandchildren and four great-grandchildren, I know some time has passed. . . . I'm not looking backward. I'm looking to the future."

I think things are looking up around here, too. Recently when Mother and I went to lunch, I actually witnessed her taking a bite of a fat-laden carrot cake with cream cheese frosting. Her face was absolutely glowing. Obviously, all the girl needed was some cake!

Now that Mother seems to be on a roll, I'd just like to say to her and Daddy, "Onward and upward! Heave ho! Get out those tennis shoes. We must never, never, never give up! Reach for the stars! Listen, the future's so bright, you guys had better buy *stock* in shades!"

"For I know the plans I have for you," declares the Lord,
"plans to prosper you and not to harm you,
plans to give you hope and a future."

JEREMIAH 29:11, NIV
∾

My Little Jaybird
Spreads Her Wings

I remember well the day I dared to pray for a daughter. I managed to get my two rambunctious boys down for a nap, then plopped down on the couch in the living room, and faced the questions I asked myself every afternoon: Should I join the boys in Slumberland, have my "Quiet Time," or run through the house like a mad woman and try to straighten it up?

But then I noticed my hope chest in the corner of the room. It had been a present to me from Scott on my sixteenth birthday. I decided to skip the nap, the quiet time, and the housecleaning and take a walk down Memory Lane. Soon I found myself sorting through stacks of memorabilia, breathing in the fresh scent of cedar, when suddenly I came across—it. I had forgotten about this delicate baby dress I had been given so long ago, and I realized that, along with the dress, I had also laid aside a dream. Now the hidden desire of my heart washed over me once again.

The story that goes with this tiny dress may be hard to believe. Before I go on, it is important that the reader keep in mind that Scott and I as teenagers were possibly the most serious-minded and lovesick to ever grace this fair planet.

The summer we fell in love we happened to be on a short-term mission trip to Central America. One afternoon in Guatemala, Scott and I visited the local market. At one booth, we stopped to watch the talented native women as they hand-stitched designs with brilliantly colored threads on exquisite articles of clothing. A tiny, simple dress caught my eye. It was obviously made for a baby girl—gauzy white cotton embroidered and fringed in a gentle blue. I looked at the adorable dress and then at Scott. He looked back at me, and before I realized what was happening, he bought the dress and gave it to me.

"Someday," he said softly, "this will look awfully cute on our little girl."

Mind you, Scott and I were fifteen and sixteen and hadn't even shared our first kiss yet, and there we were daydreaming about having a family. Wouldn't my parents have *died?*

Sitting there on the floor beside the cedar chest that afternoon with our two sons sleeping in the next room, I fingered the delicate fabric of the Guatemalan baby dress. It was a reminder of an old dream, tucked underneath my scrapbook labeled, "All My Boyfriends." (I had started the scrapbook at age fourteen, before I realized it would be all of two paragraphs long before I met my One and Only True Love.) A rush of emotion swept over me, and I began pouring my secret longings before the Lord in the form of a prayer.

Dear Lord,

You know how much I love my two boys. But this dress is so sweet and feminine! And I know Scott would kill me if I put it on Zach or Zeke. Even though I am strictly a female, I've managed to learn to mother two males made of frogs and snails and puppy dog tails. I can now hold amphibians without dropping them in disgust. I can make motorcycle noises and even play "rassle." But—there's a part of me that longs to braid hair with pink ribbons and play dress-up and have tea parties—with a child made mostly of sugar and spice. Maybe a little girl who is a miniature version of myself?

She'll probably be dark haired and outgoing, round and short—and of course she'll most likely talk the ears off a mule, just like her mother.

Oh, Lord—could I possibly have a daughter?

About ten months later, the little answer to my prayer made a grand entrance into the world. For starters, she didn't wait for the midwife, so Scott "midhusbanded" her into my waiting arms—a foreshadowing of things to come. As if by rote, Scott announced that our baby was a boy. After all, he was familiar by now with this announcement. Imagine our surprise when Mother discovered a few moments later that Scott had been quite mistaken in all the excitement, and we had been gifted with a gen-u-ine *girl!* A few weeks later I took the embroidered dress from my hope chest, slipped it onto my little doll baby, and gazed in wonder at my dream come true. Well, almost. . . .

Perhaps when the Lord formed Rachel Praise He wanted to show me that each child is His own unique creation. Or perhaps God knew that Scott couldn't handle more than one talkative brunette in this family. Whatever His reasoning, Rachel came to us with wisps of soft blond hair and an amazingly quiet spirit. May I explain that I'm not talking about the regular quiet type of "quiet." I'm talking about a semicomatose brand of "quiet." From the time our little girl was old enough to be aware of people, she developed the skill of "playing possum." Whenever someone would come over to coo over her and admire her, she'd focus her eyes straight ahead—look completely vacant—and her body would turn to stone.

The frustrating part of all this was that when Rachel was alone with me and her brothers, she would transform before our very eyes into an animated, gurgling baby. This pattern contin- ued until she was three and a half years old. She could talk my ears off as soon as a room was adult-free but stopped immedi- ately when they wandered back into her "space"—like a game of freeze tag! With adults other than myself and her grandmoth- ers, she managed to communicate by shaking her head up and down or back and forth, hoping they could understand through her brown eyes what she was inexplicably afraid to say with her mouth. It appeared to all the world, with the exception of the privileged few, that Rachel was hearing impaired. I couldn't believe it. How could any child of *mine* not want to be the life of the party?

There were *some* benefits to Rachel's quiet nature. For one, she was extremely affectionate—and portable. I could take her to any meeting and rest assured she would never utter a peep.

Though Rachel had turned out to be the silent type, do not think for a moment this meant she was clingy and afraid of adventure. When she was just a few months old, we moved to our first place in the country, our nearest neighbors were a field away. Their two teen-age daughters, Tracy and Dixie, loved to put Rachel in an open grain pail and carry her about by its handle while they fed their huge Charolais heifer, B. J.

When my baby girl reached the crawling age she often wore what I called "Sweet Pea" nightgowns. Zach and Zeke loved nothing more than to step on the hem of her sleeper, keeping her from actually covering any ground. She quickly learned to deliver the ear-splitting squeal all brothers love to hear. They also taught her to stick out her tongue on command by telling her to, "Be a sassy girl, Rachel!" How ironic. She had the gall to stick out her tongue at strangers but couldn't bring herself to say the standard "bye-bye" or "patty-cake" for the benefit of an audience.

We soon learned that, though our little daughter was the silent type, she was faster than greased lightning. She had hurried herself into the world well in advance of the arrival of the midwife and had pretty much kept right on going. Being a fast little booger and a remarkable climber, her quietness was actually dangerous at times. One cold, spring morning when Rachel was about eighteen months old, she and I enjoyed a bath together, and I had just stepped out of the bathtub with her in my arms. I wrapped her in a towel and began to fluff her dry, but before I knew what had happened, she popped out of the towel like a banana out of its peel, and shot out the bathroom door. I grabbed an old robe and ran after her in hot pursuit. By the time I reached the living room, the open front door told the tale.

I ran outside without my shoes, wet and freezing, and began to search the country landscape. As I tripped over rocks and crawled under barbed wire, I called out for my escaped toddler who was adorned this cold morning in nothing but her birthday suit. She was nowhere to be seen. My first thought was of Tracie and Dixie carting Rachel about their heifer's pen, and I felt a surge of anxiety. Surely not!

I raced to B. J.'s pen. No Rachel. I looked across the pasture and remembered the other even larger black Angus bull—and real fear gripped me! As I ran through a field of stickers in my bare feet, I tripped and felt my big toe snap. Shaking off the pain and the blood, I bolted toward the bull and found him contentedly chewing his cud, alone in the pasture. No sign of a naked baby, whole or flat.

Drained and near panic, I raced toward Dixie and Tracy's house to see if their parents might be home to join me in my search for my diminutive streaker. When I reached their back porch, breathless and broken, I was going so fast I nearly tripped over the bare-skinned and sassy little toddler sitting on the steps. There was Rachel in all her glory, her tongue sticking straight out in my direction. I decided at that moment she definitely takes after my mother!

As Rachel passed from two and then to three-going-on-four, she especially adored her daddy, and the feeling was completely mutual. We knew this—not because she *told* him so or ever actually *spoke*—but she freely offered hugs, kisses and lap-holding privileges to him. It was Scott's routine to rock her to sleep every night. They spoke not a word but were completely content with their silent cuddling ritual. Eventually, however, Scott began to long to hear the sound of his daughter's voice directed at him. For several weeks we tried everything we could think of without success, until finally the day came when we experienced the big breakthrough.

On this particular evening, Scott gathered up Rachel in his arms along with her favorite storybook and retired with her to the couch in the living room where they could be alone. His plan was to read her book and purposely mispronounce and leave out some words. We knew how Rachel hated to leave any wrong unrighted. (She still hates it!) Scott told us later what had transpired.

"Well, it was pretty slick. I started to read, and I left out some words here and mixed up others there. Rachel was in agony, shaking her head so hard her short blond hair was flying. I just kept right on reading. Pretty soon she put her face directly in front of mine and shook her head back and forth until I thought it might spin off her little neck. Finally, she could take it no more.

"'Daddy!' she blurted, 'It not *Berry* the *Moose*, it *Vera* the *Mouse!*'"

Scott paused thoughtfully and then continued with a grin, "Sweetest words I ever heard."

Slowly but surely Rachel continued to come out of her shell. By the time first grade arrived, she went unprotesting to school and to our great relief began to speak when called upon by her teachers. Now beginning fifth grade, her teachers tell me she volunteers questions and speaks right up in the classroom. However, she is still considered a quiet young lady in public with what appears to many to be a somber expression. At home, she's much more expressive.

Who knows from whence her individual personality comes? We simply love her for who she is. God answered my prayers for a daughter—but not, in His infinite wisdom, for a clone of myself. She's a unique blend of her granny's speed and sassiness, which is not without its charm. (Both Scott and my daddy insist they like their women a little on the sassy side.) With her speed, one would quickly deduce she has inherited her daddy's long legs, and he's the only one in the family who could be responsible for her strong, silent genes.

Now that she's ten, we both share a passion for reading and shopping, and she definitely shares my ability to look like an alien in the early mornings. But just as I've realized that Mother and I are not a carbon copied, twin pair of turtle doves and have had to discover for myself exactly where it is I want to soar, I suspect Rachel will be finding her own place in the sun over the next few years. That's fine with me, as long as she remembers to wear her clothes before she flies out the front door to go calling on the neighbors.

I recently spent a mother/daughter alone day with my Rachel. Lunch was indeed tastier shared with my strawberry blond daughter who has the perfect sprinkling of both freckles and giggles at this delightful age of ten. There were few silent moments. She took wonderful care of her mother, reminding me in one restaurant not to leave my purse under the table, and in another not to go off without my purchase. She still has that penchant for doing things right that caused her to blurt forth her first words to her daddy years ago. When I had to return to various stores because I kept leaving things like my sunglasses and my organizer (ha!) notebook, Rachel just shook her head and grinned.

I hope when she's all grown up we'll keep "doing lunch," and not only so that she can help me keep up with my belongings. I'd also like to have the continued joy of watching her spread her one-of-a-kind wings. Is it smothering of me to want to be around for a very long time to cheer her on, just as my mother has cheered for me?

Though finding one's individuality and separateness from Mother is an essential part of the path to adulthood, I have found there are those moments when she's simply indispensable. Those moments fall under the following categories: (1) an intensely joyful occasion, such as a wedding day or the birth of a child, (2) a time of terrible disappointment or sorrow—when you've lost your best friend or a job you desperately wanted, and (3) an in-between, boring sort of day when there's nothing much going on at all. Then you call your mom to chat about the excessive number of strings the latest batch of celery you bought happened to have or how you suddenly got tickled when you noticed that the seed wart on your index finger looked like a little old man sporting a bad toupee.

When I think of my mother's encouragement through the years (not to mention the sheer *fun* we have had together), a variety of scenes flip through my mind. I see myself at age eleven, crying in her arms about all the kids at school who weren't standing in line to be my friend. Going forward in time, I see her touching the edge of my wedding veil and telling me I am the most beautiful bride she's ever seen. I hear her voice at the birth of my first son—above the most excruciating pain I have ever felt—saying, "You're my hero, Becky. You can *do* this!" And I remember her comments as I handed her the first rough draft of a story about a crazy day with three-year-old Gabriel.

"Becky," she said, "you've got the gift. With a little help, you can get this published." Mother provided the help I needed; and after three years of writing, praying, editing, rejection, close calls, hair-pulling, and trying again, our first book—*Worms in My Tea* found a home. Upon hearing the good news from the publisher, I searched all over town for just the right card to send Mother to let her know how much she meant to me in helping to make another dream come true.

Then I found it—the perfect card. On the front was a picture of two beautiful black and white whales (I'm sure they were mother and daughter) leaping together from the foam of the bright blue ocean toward an equally blue sky. I knew Mother had seen *Free Willy* three times, and she knew *I* had always been fascinated by whales. Across the bottom of the card was written an old Swedish proverb: "Shared joy is double joy, and shared sorrow is half-sorrow."

Perhaps the saying originated from one of Scott's relatives from the old country—perhaps from a young Scandinavian mother, her blonde braids pulled back in one of those fancy knots that look like a pretzel. In my vision I see her in a long blue skirt worn under a freshly starched apron, its folds dancing in the breeze. She is sitting on a lush green hill, overlooking the North Sea, enjoying a picnic of cheese, crusty bread, and sweet goat's milk with her adorable daughter. (All people living in quaint European villages adore goat's milk, you know.) The sun sends a splash of light, just enough to illuminate the young daughter's flaxen hair, making her look almost angelic in the afternoon breeze. (Yes, I've been told I have a vivid imagination.)

Suddenly, out of the ocean, two magnificent mammals leap in unison toward the sky. Mother and child observe the miracle together. Then the awe-inspired mother blinks hard, swallows deeply, reaches across the picnic blanket, and covers the girl's hand with her own. Gazing into her daughter's deep blue eyes, the Swedish mother utters a timeless pearl that will someday be written on a perfect card beneath a picture of two black and white whales. The card will find its way to an American department store and finally, a daughter named Becky will buy it for her mother, whose name is Ruthie. The message reads, "Shared joy is double joy, and shared sorrow is half-sorrow."

Then someday, Becky will pass the saying on to her daughter, Rachel Praise, who will share it with her daughter and her daughter's daughter. And so on it will go as long as there are generations of mothers and daughters who experience the doubled delight of discovering that they are becoming more than just mother and daughter. They are becoming very good friends.

Rejoice with them that do rejoice,
and weep with them that weep.

ROMANS 12: 15, KJV

Gathering the Chicks
Under Our Wings

Throughout the centuries it is usually the daughters, mothers, grandmothers, and great-grandmothers who are the emotional heart of family genealogies. My husband's great-grandmother Peterson was the legendary matriarch of serenity and goodness in the Freeman family tree. Over twenty years ago when Scott and I first began dating, I heard epic tales from the Freeman family of their beloved Grandma Peterson.

She loved her Lord Jesus deeply and her family almost as well. She also adored cooking food so good you'd slap out your brains just licking your lips in anticipation. Just hearing stories of her scrumptious rye bread, spread with homemade rhubarb jam, made my mouth water.

Not long before Great-grandmother Peterson's death at age ninety-three, and soon after Scott and I were married, my new father-in-law, Jim, took me, Scott and his sister, Laura, on a long trip to meet Jim's beloved grandmother.

She lived in a quaint older home near where her Swedish husband had made a living from the family farm. I couldn't help thinking of the hearty immigrants from Sweden who had come to tame the wild Nebraskan soil in Willa Cather's novel, *O Pioneers!*

By the time of our visit, Grandma Peterson was just a wisp of a woman, sitting in her rocker, her tiny lap covered with an old shawl. By the soft glow of a nearby lamp, Scott and I visited with her. I knew that Grandma Peterson's only daughter Irene had died at the young age of twenty-eight, leaving behind two small boys—one of which was Jim, Scott's dad. There had been great affection between Grandma Peterson and Irene. Only after Jim was a grown man did he learn from relatives that Irene was not Grandma Peterson's daughter by blood. It had simply never crossed Grandma Peterson's mind to tell her grandson other-wise. Irene, (who had also lost her real mother at a young age) was Grandma Peterson's child through love which was, in this case, much thicker than blood. As our conversation warmed, I asked Grandma Peterson how she had ever lived through losing her daughter forty years before.

When I leaned close to hear her answer, I noticed two tears suspended on the edge of her soft, ancient eyelids.

"Honey, it was the hardest thing I ever went through," she said softly. "And I hurt so bad for little Jim and Lee, left without their mama. But with the Lord's help, life goes on." She paused, then added, "Not a day goes by I don't think of Irene, and I'm looking forward to heaven when I'll see her again."

It was then I realized that although Grandma Peterson had managed to live a full and loving life, thoughts of her Irene still brought fresh feelings of loss, pain, and love. She epitomized the expression, "There's nothing stronger than a mother's love."

I instinctively reached for her frail hand. She squeezed my fingers tightly—a wordless gesture of compassion between two generations of women with nothing, and everything, in com-mon. As our hands and hearts connected, I could almost feel myself, a supple young twig, being grafted onto the sturdy Scandinavian branches of my husband's family tree. And I realized that it is probably the love, prayers, and encouragement of mothers like Grandma Peterson that supply the lifeblood for those family trees that blossom and flourish over the centuries.

That day when I sat holding Grandma Peterson's withered hand in my young girl's hands, I could not imagine—that it could ever be possible—to be as old as this frail woman. Yet, here I am, fresh out of babies and teetering on the brink of teenage motherdom. I'm beginning to suspect how quickly the years pass. And I can see that I will someday be the matriarch in my family. For the first eighteen years of my life, I was dependent on my mother. We are now both enjoying our individual independence, but isn't it strange how short a span of time there is before mother becomes dependent on child? How deeply intertwined our lives are? How crucial to be at peace with one another?

As yet, my own mother is still vigorous, but I *feel* her passing the torch to me. She has cared for me. Someday I and my siblings will care for her. And *someday*, Rachel Praise and her brothers will care for me. And all of the painful ways we failed one another will be forgotten.

In the movie *Days of Heaven* a twelve-year-old, tongue-tied girl is one of the main characters and also the narrator. It is the story of a big brother she adores, and as he moves into one sorrowful event after another by his life choices, she often says of him, "Nobody's puhfect."

Mother and I have come to at least one conclusion as a result of writing down our experiences both as adult children and as fairly functional parents. We've about decided we don't get perfect in this life in *anything*. The best we can hope for is *better, much better,* or *mostly wonderful.* Most often, the path to *better* is to forgive, love, and accept ourselves and our family members as we are, and some of us are *very* peculiar people.

Often to our surprise, forgiveness opens the way for change leading to much better, because we find the Spirit of God has our permission to start the process of changing *us.* In other words, as we allow the Spirit to nourish us, we begin to see that we *are* being transformed into His likeness. Then the fruit begins to grow—fruits of love, joy, peace, patience, kindness, gentleness—and we may soon find that life has become *mostly wonderful.* And somewhere, deep inside ourselves, we begin to recognize the faintest image of yet another matriarch of serenity and goodness emerging to adorn our family's tree.

Thy mother is like a vine in thy blood,
planted by the waters: she was fruitful and full of branches
by reason of many waters.

EZEKIEL 19:10, KJV
❧